GREAT THEMES OF THE CHRISTIAN FAITH

GREAT THEMES OF THE CHRISTIAN FAITH

As Presented By

G. CAMPBELL MORGAN
EDWIN HOLT HUGHES
ERNEST FREMONT TITTLE
RALPH W. SOCKMAN
JOHN A. W. HAAS
WILLIAM PIERSON MERRILL
J. H. JOWETT

GEORGE A. BUTTRICK
CLOVIS G. CHAPPELL
JAMES I. VANCE
CHARLES E. JEFFERSON
ALBERT W. BEAVEN
GAIUS GLENN ATKINS
ROBERT G. LEE

EDWIN H. BYINGTON

ARRANGED BY

CHARLES W. FERGUSON

Essay Index Reprint Series

BOOKS FOR LIBRARIES PRESS
FREEPORT, NEW YORK

STANDARD BOOK NUMBER:
8369-1034-6

LIBRARY OF CONGRESS CATALOG CARD NUMBER:
68-58788

PRINTED IN THE UNITED STATES OF AMERICA

PREFACE

With the exception of the one by the late Dr. J. H. Jowett, all of the sermons included in this volume are contemporary and have not been published before. They come, for the most part, from men either now or recently engaged in the exacting work of a busy ministry and represent the normal emphasis which pastors in leading American pulpits lay recurrently upon the cardinal ideas of the Christian message. To picture these themes and the varying approaches which men in every section make to their treatment is the purpose of this book. The idea of a collection of star performers was entirely remote from anything the publishers had in mind. Nor was it their intent to offer a series of case studies in representative preaching. Rather, they hope that this book, made up as it is of sermons which are talented and at the same time preached with definite religious force and conviction, will suggest to the ministers in whose hands it falls ideas, illustrations, and methods which will be of inspiration and practical help in their own work.

CONTENTS

CONTENTS

GREAT THEMES OF THE CHRISTIAN FAITH

THE QUEST FOR JESUS

G. Campbell Morgan

"We would see Jesus."
                    John xii.21

Wide interest has been created by the announcement that G. Campbell Morgan is to join the faculty of Gordon School of Theology and Missions in Boston this Fall. Since 1919, when he came to Winona Lake, Dr. Morgan has been lecturing at Bible conferences throughout America. He was born at Tetbury, Gloucestershire, England, in 1863, was educated at Douglas School, Cheltenham, and by private study. In 1902 he received the degree of doctor of divinity from Chicago Theological Seminary. Ordained a Congregational minister in 1889, he engaged in pastoral, lecture, and Y.M.C.A. work until the time he came to America. He held a number of pastorates in England, including that of Westminster Chapel from 1904 to 1917.

Internationally known as a Bible scholar, Dr. Morgan is the author of many notable books, among which are the following: *God's Methods With Man, The Hidden Years of Nazareth, The Crises of the Christ, The Analyzed Bible* (10 volumes), *The Messages of the Books of the Bible* (4 volumes), *The Parables of the Kingdom,* and the *Ministry of the Word.*

THE QUEST FOR JESUS

"We would see Jesus."
John xii.21

These words were spoken to an apostle of Christ, Philip, by representatives of the great Gentile world, and at the end of His public ministry. So far as the Gospel of John is concerned, in chapter twelve we have the account of the last public work of our Lord. The thirteenth chapter begins,

"Now before the feast of the passover, Jesus knowing that His hour was come that He should depart out of this world unto the Father, having loved His own that were in the world, He loved them to the uttermost."

In chapters thirteen, fourteen, fifteen, sixteen and seventeen, Jesus is seen, not in public, but in private with His own disciples. In chapters eighteen and nineteen we see Him on the Cross. In chapters twenty and twenty-one we see the risen Lord. In this chapter the days of public ministry were ending, and the days of His passion rapidly approaching.

It is almost a commonplace to say that this is what people are saying everywhere today. "Sirs, we would see Jesus." Some are saying that discouraging signs abound today. I know; I live in the midst of them. But on the other hand, the age is remarkable in this fact, that everywhere people are saying in effect, "We would see Jesus." The American "Bookman" in each issue publishes two

3

lists of best sellers in the realm of books; one list in general literature, and the other in fiction. I am always interested to see these lists. A few years ago, for months, the best seller was Papini's "Life of Christ." Then for a considerable time the best seller was Bruce Barton's "The Man Nobody Knows." I am not discussing these books. I cordially dislike them both. I am simply referring to a fact. Later, among the best sellers, not having reached the head of the list, but among the first twelve is a new Life of Jesus by Emil Ludwig. The fact revealed by these sales is that men are interested in Jesus.

Again, Cecil de Mille, the producer of motion pictures, has produced nothing which made quite such an appeal to the multitude as the King of Kings. From the standpoint of a production it was marvellous, but it is a misrepresentation of the story of Jesus from beginning to end. Nevertheless anything about Jesus is attracting attention; and that is what I mean when I declare that men are everywhere saying, "We would see Jesus."

It looked ten years ago, or a little more, as though Christ would be blotted out of the world through blood and muck and misery, in a war; but as always has been the case for nineteen hundred years, He emerges and towers above all others. There is no Person in history, past, present, or in imaginative literature, who is attracting so much attention today as is Jesus.

All that being granted, such a statement both in itself, and in the fact to which it refers, needs careful consideration, because there is often a very wide difference between what humanity really needs, and what it thinks it needs; and whereas I set great value upon this interest in Jesus, and this quest for Jesus, I submit that so far as we can judge by the books I have named, by the picture I have referred to, and by a thousand other signs, the

Jesus that men want to see is not the Jesus they really need to see. The cry of humanity is often superficial, when the inspiration of the cry is profound. You remember how Tennyson in "In Memoriam" says:

> "But what am I?
> An infant crying in the night,
> An infant crying for the light,
> And with no language but a cry."

And he might have added that the crying child has no understanding of what it really needs. Crying for the light; but it does not know it is crying for the light. It is crying out of a real sense of need; but it does not understand its own need.

That is true of humanity generally. Men ask for excitement, when they need enthusiasm. They ask for solace, when they need salvation. They seek the sensual, when they need the spiritual. Everywhere men are asking for goods, when they need God. Yet the cry comes out of a need that is profound. The trouble is that men do not understand their own need.

Now, all revelation and experience teach us that God hears the cry, and He answers the need that inspires it, not man's mistaken idea of what he needs. All that is true of this quest for Jesus. Man's auto-diagnosis, man's attempt to diagnose his own condition is at fault. Everywhere men today are wanting to see Jesus, but what Jesus? The eagerness to which I have referred—and I am not undervaluing it—is the preacher's opportunity, but it creates a great and grave responsibility for the preacher, and for the Church of God. The world is saying to the Church today: We are sick and tired of listening to your debates and quarrels, and your ecclesiastical contentions. We would see Jesus.

Who is the Jesus they want to see, and Who is the Jesus that we ought to show them? The illustrations I have taken all prove the thing I have said, that men do not know what they need.

There are three clamant cries today for Him. They want Jesus as a Teacher. They admire idealism. They want Jesus as a Comrade. They are in love with His personality, and would like to find some way to pass into His friendship. They are crying out for Jesus as a Leader in social problems, and economic difficulties. It is being said on every hand that if men will obey the Sermon on the Mount, they will find the solution of the economic difficulty everywhere, and of all social problems; and this is true, but it is not all the truth. Men want Jesus in those three ways. They want to see Him as a Teacher; they want to see Him as a Comrade; they want to see Him as a Leader.

I submit that that is not the Jesus humanity needs, if that is all that is to be said concerning Him. I am not denying that He is a Teacher. He is the Teacher. I am not denying that He is a Comrade. He is the Friend. I am not denying that He is a Leader. God gave Him as a Leader and Commander to the people.

As a Teacher His social ideals are perfect. They are the ultimate ideals for the world. But if we take Him as Teacher, we must accept His teaching without qualification, as we find it in the Records. His friendship is offered us. But if we want Jesus as a Comrade, we must accept the terms of friendship as He revealed them. He is the One Who gives us the true social order. But if we want to know Jesus as a social Leader, we must discover the principles, and obey the laws He insists upon.

Now all these facts concerning Him are found in the New Testament. Invalidate it, and we have no authentic record of Him. He has been placed in human history with such definiteness of reference, as to leave no doubt in the mind of any honest person that He really lived. Tacitus, and Pliny, and Juvenal all refer to Him, but none tell you anything about Him. Josephus the Jewish writer, has told certain things about Him; but we cannot find Him personally, or as a Teacher, in Josephus. The facts about Jesus must be found by an appeal to the New Testament, and if for a moment we invalidate certain portions of it, we lose Him.

Accepting the New Testament as authentic, let us examine these matters in its light. Men want Him as a Teacher. Here then we find His teaching, and there is not a man or woman who can obey it. We cannot obey the teachings of Jesus unless or until some new power is communicated to us, enabling us so to do. I will put that in another way. We cannot obey the teaching of Jesus unless we are born again. Without the power of redeeming grace by the Holy Spirit, there is not a man or woman living on the earth who can obey His teaching. It is cheap to burn incense to the teaching of Jesus, but obedience to it is another matter. His ethic is such, that unless He gives me a dynamic, I cannot obey it. People say we want Jesus as a Teacher. But if we only have His teaching, we find ourselves unable to obey it.

Again, men want Him as a Comrade. But comradeship with Jesus is entirely impossible. The basis of friendship is unity of interest and outlook; and we lack that. We are out of touch with Him. We cannot have the friendship of Jesus, and at the same time the friendship of all that which put Him on Calvary's Cross. It is quite impossible. We cannot walk with Him and talk with Him. We should not be at home with Him. There are people in this world who would be in hell, if they reached heaven. They would be far more at home in hell than in heaven. We cannot walk and talk with this Jesus by the way, until we are one with Him in spirit. How can two walk together except they be agreed? asked Amos long ago, and it is one of the profoundest questions ever asked.

And once more. Men want Him as a Leader. They wanted Him as a Leader when He was here. They would have made Him King when He filled their bellies! He would not have it. He would not be made King on the basis of being a wholesale Food-provider. But He is King. He will set up a new social order. But the new order is the work of the Kingdom of God, and that begins by submission of the soul to God Who is King. We have no right to say in the Sermon on the Mount are certain ideals which we think will produce better conditions, unless we are prepared to obey the principles, and kiss the sceptre of the King.

Now do not misunderstand me. His teaching can be obeyed in the power of His grace. I can have Him as a Friend, so that I can say and sing, "I walk and I talk with a King." He can and will, before His work is done, set up the true social order, with all the beauties and excellence and values of the Kingdom, doing away with the damnable inequalities which are blasting the ways of men through the centuries. He is going to do all these things, because He has done something far more, something that goes far deeper, touching the root of human need.

I submit therefore that the Jesus men are clamoring for is not the Jesus of this Book, and the Jesus of the historic Church; and that is why men mutilate the Book, and dismiss historic Christianity, and attempt to insert other things in its place. Humanity's quest is the outcome of a great need; and God in Jesus, answers the cry. He is Teacher, He is Friend, He is Leader, but first He is something more than all, something profounder, something deeper.

Now let us seek the light of the context on the problem. These Greeks came, and they said to Philip,—and Philip after consulting with Andrew, brought the request to Jesus,—"Sir, we would see Jesus."

What did Christ say? In effect He said;—They cannot see Me; they cannot any more see Me, Philip, than you see Me; and they cannot and will not see Me until I am dead and risen and glorified. At the end of the thirty-sixth verse, this statement is found;

"These things spake Jesus, and He departed, and hid Himself from them."

The story begins with the request of the Greeks. It ends with the statement that He hid Himself.

Those Greeks did not see Him. Of course they saw Him in a sense. They saw the Teacher. They saw the Prophet of Nazareth. They saw the Man they had been eager to see. But they never saw Him, and nobody saw Him, until He was dead, buried, risen, glorified. If we turn over a page or two, we find that after the crowds were shut out, and He was alone with His own, Philip, this same man, in the upper room said to Him, "Lord, show us the Father, and it sufficeth us." Jesus replied, "Have I been so long time with you, and dost thou not know me, Philip? he that hath seen Me hath seen the Father." Philip did not know Him. Philip had been with Him for three and a half years. He was one of the first to follow Him. He did not know Him, had not seen Him. Peter, James, and John had not seen Him. To put it bluntly, this group knew more about Jesus half an hour after Pentecost than they knew through all the three and a half years' tabernacling with Him in the days of His flesh.

Look carefully at the story. He said, "The hour is come, that the Son of man should be glorified." What did He mean by that? I do not think another text is more generally misunderstood or misinterpreted than that. Over and over again expositors tell us that what He meant was, that the Jews had rejected Him, but the Gentiles were coming; and the hour of His glorification was coming, because the Gentile world was opening in front of Him. That is entirely false. He said, "The hour is come, that the Son of man should be glorified." What hour? What was He talking about when He said the hour is come? Have you noticed the references in John to an hour? The first is in the second chapter, in the story of Cana, and the marriage feast. His mother came and said, They have no wine. What did He say? "Woman, what is there to Me and to thee, Mine hour is not yet come." What did He mean? That His hour was not come to work a miracle? Certainly not. He did the very thing she wanted Him to do. But because of what He said to her, I know *why* she wanted Him to do it. She simply said to Him, "They have no wine." What did she want? She wanted Him to provide wine by the exercise of supernatural power. Yes, but why? Did she merely want them to have wine? Certainly not. She knew the secret of His personality, and she was eager for Him to do something through which men and the world should understand Him. She wanted Him to work a miracle, and so to reveal Himself. Jesus looked at her, and said in effect, Mother, there are things you do not know or understand. I can do what you want Me to do, but they won't see Me, "Mine hour is not yet come." What hour?

We turn over to chapter seven, and there John says they would have laid hands on Him, but His hour was not yet come. They could not do it.

We pass to chapter eight, and read that He spoke in the treasury, "as He taught in the Temple; and no man took Him; because His hour was not yet come."

Again in this twelfth chapter, "The hour is come." What hour? Go on to chapter thirteen, "Jesus, knowing that His hour was come that He should depart out of this world." Go on to chapter seventeen. He is talking to God. "Father, the hour is come." What hour? The hour of His Cross, the hour of His passion.

He said, "The hour is come." Andrew and Philip were standing there, and the Greeks, and they have expressed the desire, "Sir, we would see Jesus." Andrew and Philip break a way through, and they are in the presence of Jesus. They are looking, and they see Him. Their curiosity is satisfied, but their need is not met. Christ says, "The hour is come, that the Son of man should be glorified. Verily, verily, I say unto you, Except a grain of wheat fall into the earth and die, it abideth by itself alone; but if it die, it beareth much fruit." These men cannot see Me now. Seeing Me now, is not seeing Me. They will never see Me, until I go out into death, and out of My going into death the harvest shall spring forth for which I die. These men can only see Me through death, through resurrection, and through everything that is to follow that.

He lingered in the presence of the Cross. "Now is My soul troubled; and what shall I say? Father, save Me from this hour?" That is the hour. He said, "But for this cause came I unto this hour;" and then He said, "Father, glorify Thy name." That was His consent to the Cross. Heaven broke the silence, and then, still in the presence of the Cross, He becomes exultant. Notice the difference. First, "Now is My soul troubled," but presently, "Now is the judgment of this world; now shall the prince of this world be cast out. And I, if I be lifted up from the earth, will draw all men unto Myself." These men cannot see Me now, but if I am lifted up, I will draw them; I will draw men to Me by My Cross.

That is context, and it illuminates the text. We would see Jesus, we would like to see Him. We have heard about Him. We have heard of His works, His teaching. We would like to see Him. To which our Lord replied in effect;—They want to see Me, but they cannot see Me, save as, like a grain of wheat I go down into the ground and die. They will see Me in all that results from My death; they shall see Me in the harvest that comes out of My death and resurrection. That is His answer.

The Jesus that humanity needs is more than a human Idealist, a Man, a human Comrade; more than a human Leader. The Jesus that humanity needs is the dying, rising, reigning Christ.

Thus we find the Leader, and the Commander, and the King; when our Lord ascended, He ascended to the Throne. He is reigning, He is reigning today, and through His reign at last, the Kingdom of God will be set up, and the true social order established.

The quest for Jesus is widespread. Everywhere men are turning their eyes, attracted by something in Him that is almost irresistible. Are we showing the Jesus they think they want, or the Jesus that God knows they need? That is the question for the preacher. It is the question for the Church. It is the question for every Christian worker. God grant to us that we may see Him as He is revealed; that we may apprehend Him as the Scriptures have revealed Him. Then we can give to these men and these women who want to see Him, what they really need, the Saviour Who is able to meet their need, and satisfy their hunger; because He delivers from the power of sin.

THE CRY OF DERELICTION

George A. Buttrick

*"Jesus cried in a loud voice, 'My God, my God,
why hast thou forsaken me?'"*

Mark xv.34

Invited to deliver the Lyman Beecher Lectures on Preaching at Yale University in the Spring of 1931, Dr. George A. Buttrick, pastor of the Madison Avenue Presbyterian Church, New York, has within a brief ministry won his way to a place of commanding importance in the American pulpit. He is an Englishman by birth, a graduate of Leeds Central High School, Lancashire Independent College, Victoria University (where he received honors in philosophy), and in 1927 Hamilton College conferred upon him the degree of doctor of divinity. He was ordained into the Congregational ministry in 1915, served various pastorates of that connection, and from 1920 to 1927 was pastor of the First Presbyterian Church, Buffalo; from there he was called to succeed Henry Sloane Coffin when Dr. Coffin became president of Union Theological Seminary.

Dr. Buttrick is author of *The Parables of Jesus*, a standard work on the subject and one of the first adoptions of The Religious Book Club. A preacher and writer of exceptional force and talent, his chief excellence none-the-less lies in his pastoral work. His church, distinguished for its loyalty and zeal, is a thing of beauty which his preaching does not surpass.

THE CRY OF DERELICTION

"Jesus cried in a loud voice, 'My God, my God, why hast thou forsaken me?'"

Mark xv.34

Perhaps in some old world cathedral a guide with a group of tourists has broken across your silence by his monotonous recital. And perhaps any preaching about the Cross is to commit that sacrilege. The Cathedral of Golgotha can be trusted to speak its own message; it needs not our chatter nor the irreverent pointing of our finger. If a man must preach about it, (and sometimes he feels he must) his preaching must be the echo of his silence. It must be his penitence and his adoration crying "Behold, the man!" Such is the dictate of all: we shall try to keep it.

"The cry of dereliction," the Church has called it; and by that awful description has approached, however distantly, the desolation of the experience described.

"The cry"—piercing the silence like a knife; fear or the fire of pain become a sound. "Dereliction"—a cry strikes terror, but "dereliction" doubles and redoubles the terror. A derelict ship is one forsaken by men and by rats; in bright weather drifting helplessly, in stormy weather driven down black nights before the wind; without hand or haven or any hope; a blot on the ocean, a curse to healthy vessels, a wreck at last on some abandoned coast. "The cry of dereliction." The "most appalling sound that ever pierced the atmosphere of this

15

earth," says James Stalker. The "saddest utterance man ever made," says Nathaniel Hawthorne. Yet the Man who made it deserved not the worst of life but its best.

What are we to think of it? The Cross of Christ has focussed more earnest thought than any other event in history, but the best thought has always fallen back baffled. The profoundest theory has but touched the fringe of the crimson robe of Calvary: it has not laid hands upon its beating heart. And this cry *is* its beating heart.

What *can* we think or say? Yet these words are too vital, too real, too weighted with truth to go unpondered. Better to fail here (as fail we must) than not to try; for failure may bring us to a deeper understanding. Our lovelessness cannot interpret His love (any more than a blind man could catch the colors of the dawn), but our lovelessness may surrender to His love in the attempt. . . .

Was Jesus forsaken of God? The words of His cry are the opening words of a Hebrew psalm. People have said, therefore, that this is *not* a cry of dereliction. Jesus was harking back to a song of His nation learned in boyhood. He repeated its first words aloud and the rest of it silently for His comfort. He quietly stayed Himself upon its promises. Perhaps! . . . But the gospelists do not so understand it. They tell us that for three hours there was darkness over the whole earth. What that darkness was we do not know. Possibly a sudden storm came from the south, the aftermath of sultry heat; and possibly the poor body of Jesus was lashed by wind and sand. To the gospelists that darkness is clearly symbolical—the reflection of a blacker darkness in the soul of Christ. In that inner and outer darkness, after three hours of silence, He cried with a loud voice: "Eli, Eli, lama sabachthani." Jesus may well have found in an ancient psalm the true expression of His pain. But this cry is no mere fitting of Scripture phrases to a blood-red experience for His comfort. . . .

Was it, then, a cry of weakness? It was not a cry *of* weakness. Jesus was never weak in purpose. Even at this dread moment we cannot pity Him—we could sooner pity ourselves. But partly it was a cry *from* weakness. He had hung six hours on the Cross. His wounds were burning, His limbs cramped until any slightest movement was an agony, His blood impeded in its flow until brain and heart were like to burst, His nerves quivering. . . . Pain notoriously clouds the mind and distorts its images. This cry may have come *from* weakness, for Jesus never shrank from the penalties of the flesh.

"He saved others; Himself He could not save." Yes, in very truth! His presence had been a tonic power to weary men; but now He had no defence against is own deep weariness. A touch of His hand had healed deformed or disease-ridden bodies; but now He had no skill to close the wounds that nails had made. "He saved others; Himself He cannot save. . . . Come down from the cross that we may believe!" They might have believed if He had come down—though not for long since the eyes cannot convince the heart. We believe because He would *not* come down. He shared our human nature, and all the pains of our flesh.

Yet this cry was not mainly a cry from weakness. It came with "a loud voice": His strength was not exhausted. Later He spoke again, and with strong confidence. At the first He had refused the opiate which some-one pitying, had offered Him. The words of Browning have found their best example in Him:

"I was ever a fighter, so—one fight more,
   The best and the last!
I would hate that death bandaged my eyes and forbore,
   And bade me creep past."

But was this the *best* fight? Did He dream that the experience of death could bring such bitterness? "My God, my God, why hast Thou forsaken me?" . . . This is not a sigh of weakness. It is alive, writhing, challenging—like some lightning flash in storm over a waste land at midnight.

Then *was* He forsaken? No; for always He had done "those things that are pleasing" in God's sight. Older theologies bring outrage to any sense of right when they say (as they have actually said): "The Heavenly Father now regards Jesus as the greatest sinner to be found beneath the sun, and discharges on Him the whole weight of His wrath." Jesus was not a sinner. He had done nothing to incur God's wrath. And if God dealt with Him as if He were a sinner and the greatest sinner then we must say of God (as a cynical Frenchman *did* say of the God of these penal theologies): "our God is my devil." Never was Christ more at one with God than in the sacrifice of Calvary. He was not forsaken of God. But, so it would seem, He *felt Himself* forsaken of God. Why?

We can but grope: Was it because of some fierce, final onslaught of doubt? Being a child of woman, He was a child of questionings; for all who are born of woman are born to doubts, as the sparks fly upwards. For some the doubts are few and mild; for others they are sharp and multiplied. These latter are the honest sceptics who besiege Heaven with their oft-repeated, "Why?" The only way we can be genuinely good is to vote for goodness (and to fight for it) against a possible evil. Perhaps the only way we can have a genuine faith is to vote for it (yea, and to fight for it) in face of doubts. Faith in all of us is flecked with doubts. The converse is true: doubt in all of us is flecked with faith. The universal prayer is this: "Lord, I believe; help Thou mine unbelief." It is a poor and shallow reverence that holds of Jesus that He was free from sceptic moods. If so, He did not share our human nature. . . .

But Jesus knew the insinuation of doubt. "If thou *art* the Son of God," a devil-voice had said to Him at His temptation. He dramatized the scene in afterwards describing it, but the devil-voice really spoke from within. "Fall down and worship *me*," that voice had said.

Now on the Cross that doubt returned. "It is hardly in human nature," says Dr. Fairbairn, "to love God in death." Then—how could human nature love God in such a death? He had lived the life, that ideal life before which our best words are poor. Tennyson described it:

"Who reverenced his conscience as his king;
    Whose glory was redressing human wrong;
    Who spake no slander, no, nor listened to it;" . . .

But the life of Jesus makes such words seem foolish in their futility. He had moved as the child of God, and had blessed man (with never a lapse) by unspeakable courage and compassion. But suppose His life had been lived on a mistaken faith. Suppose His ideals had been merely a phosphorescence of the flesh, a transitory radiance dancing on a vast sea of matter. "If thou art the Son of God." . . . Suppose He was not, and suppose that God was not!

Everyone had forsaken Him—His family, His townspeople, His Church, His nation, His disciples at the last. Was life but a grim jest, as bitter as the jibes now flung at Him by evil men? Then cried Jesus with a loud voice: "My God, my God, why hast *Thou* forsaken me?" It is the only question Jesus ever put to God—and there was no answer, except a darkness over the whole earth.

"He hath been in all points tempted like as we are, yet without sin." There are times for every thoughtful man when he comes near to the perilous edge of despair. The poet who said of God:

"Closer is He than breathing, nearer than hands and feet," asked also:

> "O me! for why is all around us here
> As if some lesser god had made the world,
> But had not force to shape it as he would?" . . .

and again that same poet admitted:

> "I falter where I firmly tread,
>   And falling with my weight of cares
>   Upon the world's great altar-stairs
> That slope through darkness up to God,
>
> I stretch lame hands of faith, and grope
>   And gather dust and chaff, and call" . . .

One whose faith is always serene and strong, a shelter for the weaker faith of others, was heard to say in effect that for her the whole realm of faith is now in turmoil: she was called upon to watch her mother die in a growing infirmity—the singularly pure mind growing cloudy, the words of devotion becoming wandering, paralysis capturing the body that has always been a temple. *"Why* hast Thou forsaken me?" " *Why* died I not from the womb?", cried Job. *"Why* is all around us here as if some lesser god . . .?" We fling our "Whys" at heaven. They sound like blasphemy; but, in point of fact, only sensitive spirits of a deep compassion can thus upbraid the Almighty. There was One (made in all things like unto His brethren) who knew that agony. All the contradictions of the world conspired to nail Him to a cross. All the despairing "Whys" of the world—millions of them—joined in one vast "Why?". All the horror of a universe without God there became articulate: "My God, my God, why hast Thou forsaken Me?" . . .

But, even when that is said, we have not touched, even with a finger, the inkiest blackness of that cry. Here words fail us. Here, because of our lovelessness, we see but dimly and our words are a stammering. . . .

There is a play called "The Green Pastures." It dramatizes the primitive negro idea of the early Old Testament stories. The idea is so primitive that Heaven is conceived in terms of a fish-fry and ten-cent cigars for everybody; but ever and again that primitive thought is lit by flashes of amazing insight. A race that has learned by suffering may gain at last the crown of insight.

In that play God tries every means to break His people of their waywardness. He sends a flood, saving only one family, and thus makes a new start. He hurls His thunderbolts from the windows of Heaven upon a stubborn earth. All is without avail. Meanwhile the prophet Hosea has come to the skyey world—Hosea, the man whose wife was unfaithful to him and who won her back by silent suffering and love not to be gainsaid. And the shadow of Hosea keeps crossing the wall of that room from which God hurls His thunderbolts. Hosea does not speak. Such love as his needs no words; it is its own entreaty. God Himself begins to fear the shadow of Hosea—and that shadow (of a silent suffering) keeps crossing the wall. Is *that* the way out? Is that the weapon by which God shall win His sinful world to goodness? Must God suffer, since only God is great enough in spirit to bear the sins of the race? Everyone understands the language of love's anguish: that is the only language everyone does understand. Then must God suffer? Must He?

We cannot understand the pain of Jesus, because our lives are not pure nor are they loving. We remember the agony of our first sin, for then our lives were pure. Such was Christ's agony—for He was always pure, and He was a man, not a child; and He was Christ. We feel deeply the sin of someone dear to us—the sin and shame of husband, wife or child. We feel it deeply, because love enters to make vivid the fact. With Jesus love always entered: His compassion for mankind puts our best devotion to shame. His purity and love made sin an agony. If we were pure in heart and had compassion we might dimly understand.

"Put the thunderbolts away," God says to His archangel in that strange play. "That shadow again!" God says. "Why don't you tell him to go?" Gabriel inquires. "I cannot; I must not. God's pain—shall *that* save My people? I see a lonely Hill, and a Man toiling up it." . . . Then a voice sounds off-stage, as though all reverent humanity were speaking: "It's a terrible burden for one Man to carry." Everybody's sins! My sins! Healed not in the symptoms; healed at their deep and bitter root, by the pains of God's suffering love! Only so. . . . The Cross of Jesus was not made of wood: it was made of sin. And the sin and the doubt swept together in one awful darkness to make an eclipse of God: "Eli, Eli, lama sabachthani. My God, my God, why hast Thou forsaken me?". "It's a terrible burden for one Man to carry." . . . "In Whom we have redemption thro' His blood."

"The Cry of Dereliction?" Better to call it the "Cry of Victory." When God seemed farthest, God was nearest. When the Flower was crushed, it yielded its fragrance to the world. When Jesus felt His spirit foundering in an angry sea of doubt and sin, His feet suddenly touched solid ground. Even in His doubt there was Something to cling to; for did He not say even then: *"My God?"* There is always Something . . . or Someone! And such love as His is not cheated of Heaven. He felt Himself forsaken, but "mankind has been of another mind:" there, more than in all else that He said and did, there was God!

There He won us away from sin to Himself. We must come to Him soon or late. The sufferings of love cannot be denied. One day, perhaps this day, perhaps now, we shall shuffle off our worldliness, our selfishness; and we shall say: "It's a terrible burden for one Man to carry." Then we shall stop adding to the burden, and we shall help Him carry it.

HUMILITY

EDWIN HOLT HUGHES

One of the most universally admired bishops of the Methodist Episcopal Church, Edwin Holt Hughes, formerly president of Depauw University and an educator of distinction, is heard gladly wherever large gatherings of ministers assemble. In a sense he is a preacher's preacher, a man who goes about the presentation of the Gospel with an evident enjoyment and skill that stimulates his brothers to return to their work with renewed interest. Born in West Virginia in 1866, he was graduated from Ohio Weslyan in 1889, receiving his master of arts degree in 1892 and being ordained a Methodist minister in the same year. He holds an LL.D. both from Depauw and the University of Maine. During his presidency of Depauw from 1903 to 1908 he was actively identified with the educational program of the State, being president of State Teachers' Association, a member of the Indiana State Board of Education, and a trustee of the Carnegie Foundation.

He is the author of *The Teaching of Citizenship, A Boy's Religion, The Bible and Life, and God's Family.*

HUMILITY

I

If we were to be asked suddenly to give a definition of humility, we would doubtless be greatly embarrassed. The difficulty would be, first of all, a general one. It is never easy to become an accurate Dictionary—quickly. In the languages of the world lexicons are always a late development. Words must achieve a significance, ere the significance can be recorded: and so the meaning of a noun must be quite clear to us ere we can frame that noun in yet other words.

But the difficulty of defining is only greater when a spiritual quality is involved. A stone is easier to define than is a stony heart. To reach into the soul and pull out a mood, and then to make by words a clear picture of the mood—that surely requires a master both of the language and of the heart. The difficulty is still greater when the significance of a special word has become more or less confused by long and inexact usage. Few words have suffered more in this respect than has the word "humility." Literature itself has given us a fearful caricature. Perhaps the present generation is not well acquainted with Charles Dickens' character, Uriah Heep, whom the great author drew so vividly that the fiction seems ready to step from the pages of a novel and to insist on walking with us in spite of our protest.

Heep was ever proclaiming his humility. He bound it as a frontlet between his eyes; and, if he had possessed door-posts, he would have written it on them as a personal advertisement! He is a cringing creature—with a purpose. His effort is to crawl into the good graces of people. Those twisting hands are trying to open big doors. Those abject eyes are glancing over into a promised land. Humility was being deliberately used as a passport. It is strange and suggestive that one of the best known characters in Nineteenth Century literature should have exemplified the degradation of humility itself, should have been represented as using one of the main virtues of the Kingdom of God in order that he might gain larger areas of the devil's domain.

Dickens always protested that, while he might indulge in caricature, he did not indulge in exaggeration. We can forgive even the exaggeration if it really serves to put vice into contempt. For we soon discover that every virtue has a vice that is a close neighbor. Economy and stinginess are not very far apart. It is not always easy to distinguish between tact and deceit. Vanity may be a first cousin to self-respect. Among words and qualities the livery of heaven may be borrowed by the citizens of the other place! The wolf may adopt the clothing of the sheep; and there is good authority for saying that the exchange of wardrobes has been successful! Or, to change the figure again, the old story of the bird that flew into the lake because the waters so perfectly mirrored the blue sky represents a frequent spiritual happening.

Humility does not wholly escape this danger. We have all met more than one Uriah Heep in prayer meetings. The "worm in the dust" theology has captured many people. They appear to think that the meaner the things they can say about themselves, the more glory they may bring to God,—as if indeed the way to please the Father was to defame his children! We may well wonder how

such a perversion arose. It has no real scriptural ground.
Only once, perhaps, does the lowly metaphor of the
"worm" occur in the Bible,—and then in the case of a
prophet who had been recreant to his high calling. He
said concerning himself, "I am a worm, and no man." It
is not good, however, to take an orientalism too literally.
The prophet must have had in mind his conduct rather
than his essential nature. His humiliation came from the
fact that he had not lived up to his nature. Being a man,
he had acted like a worm; and hence came his abject
confession. So this one Biblical incident should not be
exaggerated into a gospel.

For, after all, if the Hebrew and Christian revelation
be true, we are far from being worms. We are made in
the image of God. Into us God breathed his own nature
so that we became living souls. We are destined for immortality. We are, potentially, the sons of God; and
for that very reason it doth not yet appear what we shall
be. Mrs. Browning mentions the fact that the Apostle declared that "the measure of a man" was "the measure of
an angel"; and her language does bear that lofty con-
struction. Do we overstate when we say that genuine
humility is caused by two things: the first, our faith
that we do bear the image of God; the second, that we
have marred, or even well-nigh erased, the likeness! Made
for God and his household, we have chosen the far country and the swine field. The very thing that humbled the
prodigal was the consciousness of the birthright that he
had betrayed. He had fallen far *because* he had been
high! That fact was the very reason of his abasement.

But the main emphasis now is that, whatever humility
may be or not be, it does not consist in telling falsehoods
about our essential selves. God is the God of truth; and
every spiritual quality must live with that holy attribute.

We may be utterly assured that we never recommend ourselves to Him by untrue references. Our soul is at least our nearest neighbor: and we should not bear against it a false witness. We may have "erred and strayed *like* lost sheep"; but we are not sheep! The Son of God Himself said, "How much is a man better than a sheep!" He said it not as a question, but as an exclamation. It is meaningful that the One who called men to humility called them, as well, to a recognition of their standing as sons and daughters of God. Any real evidence of the humble spirit must ever have in it these two qualities.

II

When we consider Jesus himself as our exemplar in this respect, we find the two elements appearing in his character, as they do in his teaching. He is often called "the meek and lowly Jesus." It is strange that the most powerful figure in the world's history should permit those adjectives to be applied to Himself. They are related not only to the humble birthplace in the stable-cave; and not only to the carpenter shop, in Nazareth; and not only to the unresisted cross. They are rather related to something deep in the very nature of our Lord. He does impress us as humble; and when He declares that he is "meek and lowly in heart," we feel the truth of his words.

Yet this impression of humility is in company with an impression of majesty. The Lamb of God is the Lion of the tribe of Judah. The prophecy of the Old Testament concerning the day of God's full grace was that the Lion and the Lamb should lie down together; it is not irreverent to say that they were in company in the nature of Christ. The man who was "meek and lowly in heart" cleansed the Temple of the noisy and cheating traffickers. Indeed He made claims of a peculiar personal majesty. His "I's" are impressive beyond all other words to tell. "I am the way," "I am the truth," "I am the Life," "I am the Good Shepherd," "I am the Door," "I am the Resurrection and the Life," "I and my Father are one." He made comparisons that no other man would have dared to make,—"A greater than Solomon is here," for example. Who else could have put himself beyond the wisest and most magnificent of Israel's Kings, and still have escaped the charge of individual conceit? One feels like asking—How comes it that the world persists in speaking of One who made these claims as the humble Nazarene, or as "the meek and lowly Jesus"?

This lowly One claimed empire. The world was His by a peculiar right. "All authority is given unto me in heaven and in earth." He describes all nations as being gathered before Him for the word of destiny. The student of the Bible can gather the remainder of the material for himself; it is enough now to declare that the One who was called "meek and lowly" said things about Himself and claimed things for Himself, that would convict any other person of the rankest egotism. We need not press the lesson too far, as it relates to ourselves. But we can surely say that if Christ in his amazing realm combined the humble spirit with majestic claims, we are allowed to believe that in our own tiny empires of responsibility and opportunity, we can be humble without being abject and powerless. "A broken and emptied vessel" is not the final symbol of humility.

On the other hand, the vessel that would boast of its grace, and beauty, and fulness as if they were self-conferred, is not the token of the Kingdom. When the potter finds the clay and does the molding, he is entitled to his praise. Evidently there were three classes whom Jesus rebuked most sharply—the hard-hearted, who neglected kindly social duties; the materialistic who put their dependence upon the coarser things of life; and the self-sufficient who took to themselves credit for their "gifts" and ascribed not glory to the Author. Perhaps his words about the last-named class were the most severe. Once he scorched his way through many verses of indictment,—with phrases that were piercing indeed. "Ye generation of vipers." "Ye serpents." "Ye whited sepulchres." "Who hath warned you to flee from the wrath to come?" Yet the persons to whom He spoke thus were not bad people in their usual conduct. They did tithe. They did fast. The Pharisee in the parable did not lie about himself. The tale of his mere behavior was doubtless true. The difficulty was that he assigned credit to his own merit and power. He travelled by the throne of God as the most appropriate road to his own heart! He came near to the Altar but was very far from the Altar's God.

Humility, therefore, must always be the recognition of our dependence. The question is for each, "What hast thou that thou hast not received? This drives us back to the givers, and to the Giver. It is often said in outworn witticism that the difficulty with the so-called self-made man is that he worships his Maker! The truth is that there is no self-made man. Any honest appraisal of one's self will quickly show that fathers and mothers, friends and teachers, and God Himself have been the givers of real life to us. We have done something, and given something. Yet, if we keep our books on both sides of the ledger, we shall always find a big balance of debit recorded against us. The gifts we have received are so many more and so much greater than the gifts we have conferred. Where then is boasting? The crime of the Phari-

see is that he sins against the essential facts of life. The
lack of humility always stands for falsehood. Self-satis-
faction is always a liar! Humility is truthfulness.

With all this in mind, we can understand Jesus' indig-
nation against the pride that swaggered over its own
character or strutted before its own achievement. Usually
the trouble is that, the great Babylon that we think we
built, we did not build in any large part. God made the
materials. He provided for us, also, a thousand partners.
All true cathedrals of the soul represent a company that
no man can number. They stand for centuries of cooperat-
ing spirits. When at last the capstone is placed, the cry of
"Grace! Grace!" is always appropriate. Even a Christo-
pher Wren is never alone. The glory of St. Paul's is from
God, as it is to God. If humility does not mean a false
depreciation of our nature so that the verdict becomes an
untruth, neither does it mean a false appreciation of our
character and work, so that the verdict again becomes an
untruth. Humility does mean the recognition of the fact
that life itself is the gift of grace; and that when our
thought travels upward along the path by which that gift
comes, the goal is always God.

III

It should be quite apparent that humility is more than
an abstract virtue. If it involves the acknowledgement of
facts as they are, it must have a real relation to success.
We cannot think it possible that a genuinely efficient life
could be based on falsehood. It was just here that the
Romans failed. They had little room for the passive virtues. If you had said to them, "The meek shall inherit the
earth," they would have deemed you less than half-wise.
Their theory was that the fierce would capture the world.

It is an evidence of the power of Christ that against all of the assured conviction of his earthly time He still succeeded in exalting the lowly spirit. He took such words as meekness and humility and lifted them out of the mud and gave them a place among the stars. Occasionally in wider areas there is an evidence that Jesus was wiser than all the teachers of violence. In America we have had a striking contrast between two races,—the red race and the black race. The Indian has not been noted for his meekness. He had his undoubted wrongs, and he met them with a fierce and unyielding mood. He dashed himself against forces that he could not overcome. Slowly he was driven from one desert to another, from one mountain pass to another, until at last, a constantly dwindling factor, he found himself defeated. On the other hand, the negro bore his outrages with a docile spirit. He humbly met his reverses, smiled at his persecutors, and walked his obscure path with cheerful feet. The figures, whether of property or education, plainly show that the colored people have made about as remarkable a racial advance as the world's history can show. Their humility has been far more than a cloak against the cold winds of adversity: it has been power for making progress against those winds. In the presence of difficulties and sorrows the negro found himself singing, "steal away to Jesus"; and when he did so, he found that Christ was not only a refuge; He was strength. There can be no questioning of the fact that the humility of the negro race has been a considerable factor in its amazing development. Its meekness has helped it to inherit an ever increasing section of the earth.

All the above would appear to indicate that humility stands for more than a distinctly religious principle,—if we may for a moment adopt a rather bungling division of life. The humble spirit represents a universal law. Many men feel that the demand for the lowly spirit is an example of divine arbitrariness, and that it stands for God's will for personal rulerships. In truth, the feeling is that humility is merely a preacher's word and that it has no effect beyond the sanctuary. But duly we discover that the garment of life is like that taken from Christ on the day of the Cross; it is woven throughout and is of one piece. If humility is really good in religion, it is good for all of living.

It has its social side. Long ago George Eliot wrote, "I never pity conceited people; they carry their own comfort with them." Perhaps God feels somewhat like that,—only in a more compassionate way. Surely men feel as the great authoress did. The conceited man shuts himself away from human sympathy, even as he deprives himself of the divine companionship. He that inhabiteth eternity dwells with the humble and contrite heart,—because no other kind of a heart will feel the need of admitting Him.

It would not be hard to show that the law of humility has its intellectual side. Years ago a great teacher said of one of his students: "I think that he will make a real scholar. He is genuinely humble." Any instructor will tell you that the most difficult pupil is the most conceited pupil. Why should one struggle for that which one already has,—in his own estimate? A great scientist once declared that nature whispered her secrets only to the humble mind; while a business man said a like thing about his class,—that the successful man in commerce was the one who knew how to face his losses as well as his gains! More than one man has failed because his vanity would not allow him to deal frankly with the debit side of his account books. Indeed, it could readily be shown that there is no way of living where the lesson of humility does not have its value. Life may be defeated at any one of its points by the wrong kind of self-confidence. The words, "He that humbleth himself shall be exalted; and he that exalteth himself shall be abased," are not the slogan of the mere mystic or mediaevalist. They are, on the contrary, the wisdom of God, the timeless counsel to all the sons of time.

Unless we are humble enough to feel our need of God, how can He come to us? Will the great Lord force Himself upon the unwilling spirit, break down the door that is closed by the hand of an inner satisfaction? Surely not! So it comes to pass that the virtue which is so difficult to define is even more difficult to cultivate. Humility comes to our hearts only when we view the chasm that stretches between us and the Holy Lord,—only when we send our hearts across it in dependence and petition. When we do that we shall always go down to our houses justified, to our characters glorified, and to our work sanctified. The Damascus Roadway to discipleship and apostleship begins with the humble question, "Lord, what wilt thou have me to do?"

THE BELATED PREACHER

Clovis G. Chappell

"All the baptism he knew was that of John."
Acts xviii.25 (Moffatt)

Clovis G. Chappell, a master of character delineation, is known throughout America for his able books of sermons. Beginning in 1922 he has published *Sermons on Biblical Characters*, *More Sermons on Biblical Characters*, volumes on Old and on New Testament characters, and in 1930 he issued a series, *The Sermon on the Mount*. In a very real sense the success of his books has paralleled the fruitfulness of his ministry, for his sermons are marked by a warmth of sympathy which appeals to men in every walk of life. Throngs flocked to hear him during his pastorate of the Mount Vernon Place Church, Washington, D. C. His ministry at the First Methodist Church, Memphis, Tennessee, saw the incoming of hundreds by conversion at regular services and the strengthening of the whole work of the Church. He has recently been appointed to the First Methodist Church, South, Houston, Texas.

Dr. Chappell was born in Tennessee in 1882. He received his preparatory education in the Webb School at Bell Buckle, Tennessee, and continued his studies at Duke and at Harvard. In 1920 both Duke University and Centenary College conferred upon him the degree of doctor of divinity.

THE BELATED PREACHER

"All the baptism he knew was that of John."
Acts xviii.25 (Moffatt)

"All the baptism he knew was that of John." This is a rather surprising and startling statement to read of one who has been instructed in the things of the Lord. It becomes even more so when we realize that the one so instructed has accepted that instruction and has actually become a disciple of Jesus. And while the spiritual requirements for the pulpit are no greater than those for the pew, it becomes more surprising still, when we realize that this man has not only become a disciple, but has entered the Christian ministry. Yet, such is the case. Apollos is a preacher. He is one of the great men of the early Church. He has set himself to the tremendous task of remaking men and of bringing in the Kingdom of God. But, sad to say, he undertakes this amazing impossibility knowing only the baptism of John. What inadequate equipment! How can he hope for anything better than heart-breaking failure? He has much, but it is not enough.

(I) Look at the wealth of his equipment.

1. He was a man of great native gifts. Now, we are not forgetting the fact that the bulk of the world's work must be done by us who are of mediocre ability. Nor are we forgetting that the man of one talent is just as worthy of honor as the man that has five. No man is to be crowned simply because he is gifted. Large gifts do not

reflect credit upon the receiver, but upon the Giver. But while this is true, it is also true that vast ability opens the door to vast usefulness. A consecrated million will surely do more than a consecrated penny. Therefore, we are glad to welcome into our brotherhood this man of outstanding ability. And we rejoice that through the centuries so many of the world's greatest intellects have consecrated their large gifts to the service of the Kingdom.

2. He was a man of fine culture. He was a native of Alexandria. This city, like the native city of St. Paul, was the seat of a university. It also possessed the greatest library of antiquity. It was a city of scholars and philosophers. Apollos had been exposed to the finest educational opportunities of his day. Not only so, but he had made wise use of those opportunities. He brought to the work of the ministry one of the best trained minds of his day. Thus splendidly equipped by nature and training, he was able to preach even in the pulpit of the marvellously endowed and cultured Paul and to share laurels with him. Such a preacher would be capable of winning a hearing in any age. In fact, Apollos, Paul and Luke share the honor of being the three best trained men of the early Church.

3. He was a man of flaming zeal. He kept the hot fires of a fine enthusiasm burning upon the altar of his soul. That is splendid. The truly worthwhile work of this world is ever done by the hot-hearted. It is these, too, who call out the best there is in us. The tepid, timid, half-hearted individual does little, and makes little appeal to either God or man. And the burning ardor of Apollos is all the more dynamic because it is coupled with high culture. Unfortunately, outstanding scholarship and flaming zeal do not always walk arm in arm. There are those the chief ends of whose learning seem to be either

to serve as a new kind of fire extinguisher or for cold storage purposes. Of course, this is not the fault of scholarship. Certainly, we are not to conclude that the fine flower of zeal thrives only in the lean soil of ignorance. We have all known those who were at once dreadfully lacking both in knowledge and also in zeal. Hot enthusiasm is good in any worthy cause, but the more intelligent it is the better. Therefore, we appreciate especially the zeal of Apollos.

4. He was mighty in the Scriptures. How refreshing! No disciple who aspires to a vigorous spiritual life can afford to neglect the Bible. Certainly no one who teaches in the Church School or holds a position of leadership in the Church can afford to slight this supreme book of mankind. But the Bible is the preacher's specialty. He is expected to be able to teach it with some degree of assurance and authority. Apollos had studied and read widely, but he had majored on the word of God. Therefore, Luke could write of him that he was mighty in the Scriptures. We congratulate him and we congratulate those who were privileged to sit under his ministry. It is well for the preacher to be mighty in organization, mighty in financiering, but it is better still for him to be mighty in the Scriptures. It is such men whose ministry has ever been most rich in abiding usefulness. Bunyan has guided millions toward the celestial city. This he has done, not simply because he was a genius at Allegory, but more still because he was mighty in the Scriptures.

5. He was hospitable to the truth. He was eager and ready to learn from any who were able and willing to teach. That was his salvation. That is what kept him from squandering his fine resources for returns meager in quantity and poor in quality. Being eager to learn, he was, therefore, capable of teaching and preaching. To

close the door of the mind is fatal. Years ago I knew a
young man of high promise who decided to enter the ministry. His educational opportunities were of the very best.
His work both in college and seminary was full of promise. But having finished and entered upon his chosen
work he seemed to think that his days of toil were over.
He quit reading, he quit growing. He became a victim
of arrested development, a disappointment to himself and
to others.

Apollos was different. He continued to learn and, therefore, to grow. And what is more commendable still, he
was willing to learn about his own specialty and that from
those who were doubtless far his inferiors both in ability
and culture. Surely a rare man was Apollos. Were I serving on the committee for securing a new pastor for the
Church of which I was a part, I should give careful
consideration to this gifted, cultured, zealous open-
minded, Scriptural preacher. But having considered, I
should have to vote against him, that is unless I was very
sure he was going to advance. This is true because Apollos
had one great defect that, if left uncorrected, must cause
his brilliant ministry to be little better than a failure.

(II) What was wrong with Apollos?

It was not that he was a heretic. He had not been im-
properly instructed, he had been inadequately instructed.
All the baptism he knew was that of John. He did not
know the baptism of the Spirit. He had not entered into
that life-giving, transforming experience that had come to
his fellow disciples at Pentecost. He was thus belated,
completely behind the times spiritually. He had not ar-
rived. He was not in the finest and fullest sense a Christian at all. Therefore, in spite of all his lordly gifts, in
spite of his commendable zeal, he was but poorly
equipped for the great work of the ministry. No man is

adequate for the task of Kingdom building whose adequacy is not of the Holy Spirit.

This is the plain teaching of our Lord. "It is the Spirit that quickeneth." How well fitted were Peter and John after they had seen their risen Lord. They had companied with Him during the days of His earthly ministry. They had seen Him die. They had seen His tomb which was at the same time the grave of their dearest hopes. Peter had looked upon this grave with increased bitterness because of his cowardly denial. But a new day dawned. It was Easter. Christ had risen—the same forgiving Savior as of old. He had sent a special message to Peter and had granted him a private interview. The past was buried and Peter has a wonderful story to tell. His fellow disciples share his eagerness. But Jesus says "Not yet, wait for the promise of the Father. Tarry ye till ye be endued with power from on high."

And just as it is true that no man is adequate without this experience that Apollos lacked, it is equally true that to all who claim it there comes an amazing adequacy. We think wistfully at times of the privileges of those early friends of Jesus. How wonderful to have walked by His side, to have felt the touch of His hand, to have sat under the spell of His voice. No wonder that their hearts were crushed when they found that he was going to leave them. No wonder that they could not think of the empty, gray days ahead without their faces being wet with hot and bitter tears. But Jesus tells them in His quiet way that by going He is doing the best possible for them. "It is expedient for you that I go away." "My going is the roadway to an infinite nearness." And, incredible as it seemed, they found it gloriously true. They realized after Pentecost that He was not only with them, but within them, and that their sufficiency was of Him.

"All the baptism he knew was that of John." What a fatal defect, what a tragic loss! For this means that though he knew about Jesus, he did not know Jesus Himself. He knew about Him, but he did not realize Him. He could not say with Paul, "Have I not seen Jesus Christ, our Lord." He could not shout with him with unshaken and unshakable conviction, "I know whom I have believed and am persuaded that He is able to keep that which I have committed unto Him." He knew the facts about Jesus, but Jesus was not a reality to his own heart. This was true because the Spirit was not yet able to take the things of Christ and to show them to him.

Lacking the Spirit, he had no power to reproduce Christ. He had not become a new creation. He could not say, "For me to live is Christ." He could not sing, "I am crucified with Christ, nevertheless I live, and yet not I, but Christ liveth in me." Men did not take knowledge of him that he had been with Jesus. Wanting the Spirit, though he sought to imitate Christ, he could not incarnate Him. He was simply undertaking to do in the energy of the flesh what can only be done in the power of the Spirit.

Of course, this sad defect told upon his entire ministry, upon his personal contacts and upon his preaching. He was an eloquent and forceful preacher. Those who heard him were instructed. They were doubtless thrilled and entertained. They were compelled to admire the fine qualities of the preacher. But he somehow failed to bring them a sense of the presence of Christ. He did not compel them to say in their hushed and awed hearts—"Surely, God is in this place." Therefore, though a wonderfully attractive preacher, he was not a powerful preacher.

It is evident that those choice saints, Aquila and Priscilla, were disappointed in him. They went to the service that day, no doubt, with high expectancy. But the preacher had hardly begun till they found that there was something lacking, and they were very sure what that something was. In his ministry to the saints, he was thoroughly disappointing. Nor was he more successful with those without the Church. We have no right to say that those twelve backward disciples that Paul found upon his visit to Ephesus were converts of Apollos. Probably they were not. But at least they had this in common with this great preacher, they were entirely ignorant of the baptism of the Holy Spirit.

Now, many years have passed since then, so many that we are now celebrating the nineteen hundredth anniversary of Pentecost. But after all these centuries, we cannot shut our eyes to the fact that there are vast numbers today that are just as far behind the times as was Apollos. In fact I am afraid that Apollos would feel far more at home among a group of modern saints than among those of whom he was a part. It is my very firm conviction that the saddest lack of the Church today is that from which Apollos was suffering. We need his ability and culture, but there must be something more. If I were asked to point out the greatest weakness of the pew today, I should have to say "A lack of a vital spiritual experience." If I should be asked to indicate the greatest weakness of our increasingly efficient teaching force, I should have to answer, "lack of a vital spirituality." If I should be asked the same question with regard to our ministry which is the best trained the Church has ever had, I should have to give the same answer. Too often we as Apollos are undertaking in the energy of the flesh what can only be done in the power of the Spirit.

(III) Was there a way out for Apollos? Is there a way out for us? I am perfectly sure that these questions may be answered in the affirmative.

Look at Apollos. The service over Aquila and Priscilla do not pass the word along that the preacher is unsafe and that the people had better refuse to give him any further hearing. Had they done so they might have worked a great injury both to the preacher and to the congregation. Instead they did that which indicated both consecration and the highest order of tact. They invited the preacher home with them and expounded unto him the way of the Lord more perfectly. That is magnificent. It is hard to tell which to admire the more, the instructors or the instructed. It is certainly a delicate matter to instruct a preacher, for we are a sensitive tribe. Great credit is certainly due these tactful teachers. But great credit is also due Apollos. He did not flash his diploma and his various degrees at them. Instead he listened with childlike humility. As he listened, his heart burned within him. He understood and claimed.

A little later we meet him again in the City of Corinth. We do not know as much about his work here and later on as we should like. But of this we feel confident—from this time his ministry took on new effectiveness and power. The record says that he helped them much who believed through grace. He was now not only an eloquent and learned preacher, but better still he was a helpful preacher. And the experience that came to Apollos is also for you and me. "This spake he of the Spirit which they that believed on Him were to receive. 'For the promise is unto you, and to your children, and to all that are afar off, even as many as the Lord our God shall call.' "

THE KINGDOM OF GOD

Ernest Fremont Tittle

Since 1918 Ernest Fremont Tittle has been pastor of the First Methodist Church, Evanston, Illinois. During his ministry at the seat of Northwestern University he has maintained Sunday after Sunday the respect, attention, and support of students and faculty. He does it not by preaching on zoology but by a fearless proclamation of the Gospel. He is splendidly aware of the contemporary but equally convinced of the eternal. His latest book, *The Foolishness of Preaching,* announces as clearly as anything could the straightforward and uncompromising message which he has always brought. He serves on the faculty of Garrett Biblical Institute and is frequently in demand as a college preacher throughout the east and middle west.

Born in Springfield, Ohio, in 1885, Dr. Tittle was graduated from Ohio Weslyan in 1906 and later from Drew Seminary. He held successive Methodist pastorates in Christiansburg, Dayton, Delaware, and Columbus, Ohio. His first book, *What Must the Church Do To Be Saved?* was published in 1921. *The Religion of the Spirit* appeared in 1928.

THE KINGDOM OF GOD

What was the supreme interest which Jesus had in life? The question admits of but one answer, "The Kingdom of God"; a divine-human society in which men in every walk of life would be eager to know and to do the will of God, and in which every human relationship would be governed by the spirit of good will. Jesus never doubted that the Kingdom of God would come. He hoped that it would come soon, in his own lifetime in fact; and in this hope he was destined to be disappointed. But he died believing that a divine-human society would some day appear upon this earth. On the last night of his life, when he gave the cup to his disciples, he said to them, "Take this and divide it between yourselves, for I say unto you that I shall not drink henceforth from the fruit of the vine until the Kingdom of God shall come."

Believing in the possibility of a diviner civilization, Jesus made the securing of it the supreme purpose and passion of his life. The New Testament makes it abundantly clear that whenever the Kingdom of God was concerned Jesus was absolutely uncompromising, even when he realized that for him personally the alternative to compromise was crucifixion.

Now, when it comes to this supreme interest of Jesus the feelings of most of us are mixed. We sometimes feel like asking, and in our hearts we do ask, What is the good of it all, this brave pursuit of a goal that is never reached, this valiant striving for a Kingdom that never comes? The Charge of the Light Brigade was magnificent

49

but it was not war. And this idealistic quest of a Kingdom of God—it too, no doubt, is magnificent; but is it common sense? So sometimes we ask and think. But we are obliged to acknowledge that there *is* something magnificent about it; and, occasionally, the question comes, Would you be willing to have that kind of magnificence die out of the world in which you and your children are obliged to live?

Suppose that it had never appeared in the world. The favorite device of Francis Bacon was a ship sailing between the Pillars of Hercules into an unknown sea and above it the legend, "More Beyond." Suppose that neither Francis Bacon nor any other man had ever become enamored of such a device; that instead the whole race of men had chosen as its emblem a ship at anchor and over it the legend, "Nothing More or Better to be Expected." Suppose that from the beginning until now people had been content with present achievements, or had at least been incurably skeptical as to the possibility of any great human achievement. Suppose that the race had produced no prophets, no idealists, no pioneers, no persons who in the eyes of their contemporaries appeared as mad men and fools. Where and what would we be today? We are obliged to acknowledge that human idealism, with its perpetual challenge, has kept the human race from becoming as stagnant as a scum-covered pool.

Nor is this the only acknowledgment which we find it necessary to make. This idealistic quest of a Kingdom of God has been not only magnificent; to at least some extent it has been effectual. Twenty-six hundred years ago a Hebrew prophet looked and labored for the coming of a day when the nations would beat their swords into plow-shares and learn war no more, and it does not need to be said that the day of his vision has not appeared.

But was that prophetic expectation and passion altogether in vain? For answer, look at the League of Nations, a Permanent Court of International Justice, the Briand-Kellogg Pact, and the address delivered on Armistice Day by the President of the United States. The early Christians expected to see a heaven on earth. They expected to see it before they died. They did not see it or anything approximating it. But was even that expectation altogether in vain? Who can believe that it was when he considers how that early Christian vision of a holy city, a new Jerusalem, coming down out of heaven from God, has haunted the minds of some men in generation after generation and is, today, making it impossible for a growing number of people to be content with the slums of London and the corruption of Chicago.

One of the earliest responses to William Lloyd Garrison's appeal for the immediate emancipation of negro slaves came from a theological school in Cincinnati, Ohio. One hundred and ten students of this little known theological seminary signed a statement which said that they were in hearty accord with the position which was being taken by Mr. Garrison and that they would do everything in their power in support of it. Whereupon, the Lane Theological Seminary appeared on front pages all over the United States! It seemed as if everybody knew that up (or down) in Cincinnati, Ohio, there was a theological school whose students had gone crazy. In the North as well as in the South the school was assailed as a hotbed of abolition. Pressure was brought to bear upon the Board of Trustees, who finally weakened and forbade the students to discuss the question of slavery even in private. What happened? Eighty of the one hundred and ten students withdrew from the seminary and went hither and yon proclaiming the gospel of immediate emancipation.

In city after city, when one of them turned up, people scornfully said, "Behold this dreamer cometh." But some of those young men lived long enough to see their dream come true.

We know that human idealism is not only magnificent but creative. We know that slowly but surely, and not always slowly,* it brings certain desirable things to pass. We therefore hope that at least a few of our contemporaries will choose for themselves the rôle of idealist. We should dread to think that nobody in our generation would make the securing of a nobler civilization the supreme purpose and passion of his life. But when it comes to ourselves—well, our own position in this matter might be somewhat inelegantly but accurately stated in the current and all too popular suggestion, "Let George do it." We want very much to have somebody *else* sail through the Pillars of Hercules into an unknown sea in quest of the Kingdom of God. It does not seem to occur to us that in refusing ourselves to sail we are likely to miss something that is tremendously worth while. So let us consider some of the results in personal experience which any earnest attempt to build on earth the Kingdom of God appears able to produce.

One of them is an inspiring sense of fellowship with the noblest spirits of the race and particularly with the noblest of them all. Consider for example the romantic story of Albert Schweitzer, one-time professor in the University of Strassburg, a profound scholar, a brilliant writer, a distinguished musician, probably the greatest living expounder and interpreter of Bach. He publishes an epoch-making book, entitled "The Quest of the Histori-

* The idea of outlawing war, advanced less than ten years ago by a private citizen of Chicago, has now received the official endorsement of more than sixty of the leading nations of the world.

cal Jesus," in the writing of which he comes to the con-
clusion that it is quite impossible to rediscover the Jesus
of history by the methods of scholarship alone; that,
however competent your scholarship may be, your quest
of the historical Jesus is doomed to fail unless you develop a spirit akin to His own. So what does he do?
Already thirty years of age, with an assured position in
the world of scholarship, he decides to study medicine
with a view to going to Africa as a medical missionary!
He is convinced that one way to develop the spirit of
Jesus is to respond, as Jesus did, to human pain and need,
of which there is a vast deal in Africa. He gives up his
professorship, goes to a medical school, and graduates
from it. Then he gives organ recitals in the hope of
raising enough money to finance his African adventure,
adding to the money thus raised the proceeds of the sale
of his great book on Bach. Finally, in the spring of 1913,
accompanied by his wife, who has taken training as a
nurse, he sails for the River Ogowe, in Equatorial Africa,
where nine years later he writes:

"The operation is finished, and in the hardly lighted
dormitory I watch for the sick man's awaking. Scarcely
has he recovered consciousness when he stares about him
and ejaculates again and again: 'I've no more pain! I've
no more pain!' . . . His hand feels for mine and will
not let it go. Then I begin to tell him and the others who
are in the room that it is the Lord Jesus who has told the
doctor and his wife to come to the Ogowe, and that white
people in Europe give them the money to live here and
cure the sick negroes. Then I have to answer questions
as to who these white people are, where they live, and
how they know that the natives suffer so much from sick-
ness. The African sun is shining through the coffee
bushes into the dark shed, but we, black and white, sit

side by side and feel that we know by experience the meaning of the words: 'And all ye are brethren' (Matthew 23,8). Would that my generous friends in Europe could come out here and live through one such hour!"

Would it be worth while to live through one such hour of sacrificial ministry to human need and of inspiring fellowship with the noblest and greatest spirit that has ever appeared in our human world? Does the possibility of such an experience make any appeal to you and me? Let us compliment ourselves to the extent of assuming that it does; then let us dare to face the fact that unless and until we ourselves undertake to do something which has a dash of idealism in it we shall never live through one such hour.

Another result in human experience which comes of devotion to the Kingdom of God is the discovery of God himself. In a fascinating book entitled "South," Sir Ernest Shackleton has told the story of his ill-fated attempt to cross the South Polar continent from sea to sea. His ship, called curiously enough in the light of what happened, "The Endurance," was caught between pressure ice and slowly ground to death. For weeks he and his men drifted about on floating ice and then, when their ocean camp site broke up, they took to their small boats in the stormiest and most treacherous of seas. Their food supply reduced to such an extent that they were glad to eat blubber, fried, boiled, or even raw, they landed at last upon a little island, far out of the way of South Sea traffic, where their chance of being rescued was just nothing at all. So Sir Ernest and two others made a last desperate attempt to reach a whaling station in South Georgia. They succeeded. And the gallant leader of this forlorn hope declares that during the long, racking march of thirty-six hours over the unnamed mountains and glaciers of South Georgia it seemed to him often that he and his two companions were not three but four. He said nothing on this point to the others; but when the goal was reached one of them said to him, "I had a curious feeling on the march that there was another person with us."

Now, arm-chair psychologists may attribute an experience of this sort to tense nerves, to the awful sense of loneliness that is begotten by the vast silence of an antarctic waste, or to any other non-religious cause which inexperience of the deeper side of reality may suggest to them. They may put it down in their notebooks as an illustration of the susceptibility even of strong and intelligent natures to strange hallucinations. But, over against this all too facile explanation of a great experience, there is the testimony of thousands of men who, engaged in heroic quests, braving in the name of some ideal the wrath of the elements or the wrath of men, have had the conviction that they were not alone, that God was with them. A young Methodist clergyman to whom, more than to any one else, was due the settlement, on a fairly just basis, of the last strike in the Colorado coal fields, who rallied to his support nearly every leading newspaper of the state, shamed its governor out of a perfectly untenable position, stood on the one hand against the ruthlessness of some of the coal operators and, on the other hand, against the resort to violence advocated by some of the strike leaders,—this man told me quite simply that what he did and endured during those tense and terrible weeks brought to him his first great experience of God.

Some of us who believe that there is a God but who not once in all the years have had any indisputable experience of God wonder not a little why we have not. The reason may be that not once in all the years have we really risked anything in the name of an ideal. We have yet in utter abandon to give ourselves to any worthful cause.

Still another personal gain which comes through devotion to the Kingdom of God is something to live for. When we say of some man that he has not yet found himself, what do we mean? We mean in part that not yet has he discovered what he is good for, what he is peculiarly fitted to do in the world. He is spoiling a good business man by trying to teach or preach. Or perhaps he is spoiling a good teacher or preacher by trying to make a go of business for which he has no qualifications. But when we say of some man that not yet has he found himself, do we not also mean that not yet has he found something to live for, some thing to which he may enthusiastically devote himself and thus secure unity in his own soul, that integration of personality which produces power because it enables a man to concentrate all of his faculties on the task which he has chosen or which (he himself may feel) has chosen him.

It is a significant fact that when a man finds something to live for he does not sell his birthright for a mess of pottage, or the possibility of intellectual leadership for a cup of transient pleasures, or the possibility of a great happiness for a "wild night." He does not squander his leisure upon pursuits that are trifling or dissipate his energies in ways that are unrewarding. But notice this: A man may choose an object in life which in his own eyes appears big enough to command him, but which is not big enough to lift him out of himself. Here is a man who sets out to become a millionaire. He believes that a million dollars represents an object that is big and worthful enough to command him, and it does command him. It organizes him, unifies him, keeps him from becoming a house divided against itself. In a way, it accomplishes for him what religion is supposed to accomplish; it secures for him a certain integration of personality. *He* does not squander his leisure on trifling pursuits. *He* does not dissipate his energies in ways which, from his point of view, are unrewarding. He becomes a man of power, a man to be reckoned with, a very considerable force in the community in which he lives. What, then, if any, is the objection to the selection of a million dollars as a goal for human endeavor? This: A million dollars is not an object big enough or worthful enough to lift a man out of himself, and so to fortify him against personal disappointments and misfortunes by giving him a concern which transcends them.

On his return to Washington after Lee's surrender, Abraham Lincoln opened his Shakespeare and read aloud the lines,

> "Duncan is in his grave;
> After life's fitful fever he sleeps well.
> Treason has done his worst; nor steel nor poison,
> Malice domestic, foreign levy, nothing
> Can touch him further."

But concerning Lincoln himself let it be noted that before he was in his grave he was measurably fortified against personal griefs and disappointments. He had found a cause that was great enough to lift him out of himself and enable him to forget himself. Even when his beloved Willie died, although he was terribly shaken, he managed to pull himself together in response to a cause which he held to be of more consequence than his own grief. His domestic life was none too happy, but even above its irritations he managed to rise in obedience to the summons of a great human need.

A concern that transcends all personal interests; a cause that is, and is considered to be, of more consequence than any personal ambition or personal hope, even of happiness—without that a man is cruelly exposed to the slings and arrows of outrageous fortune, pitifully subject to the vicissitudes of life. The Kingdom of God is something which society needs; it is also something which the individual needs to take him out of himself and enable him to forget himself.

Some years ago, Professor William James captured the attention of the world by suggesting that what we now need to do is to discover "a moral equivalent of war, something heroic that will speak to men as universally as war does and yet be compatible with their spiritual selves as war has shown itself to be incompatible." Well, the Kingdom of God offers all the requirements for a moral equivalent of war. It is, to begin with, something heroic, something which offers to a man all the opportunity that he needs for the display of heroism. Not long ago, a distinguished American was saying that in order to maintain the virility of the race we need a good sized war at least once in every generation. Utter nonsense! War, as we now know, becomes a terrific biological drain through its destruction of the most virile of human stocks. An infinitely better means of maintaining human virility would be provided by devotion to the Kingdom of God.

In any list of the half dozen bravest men of the thirteenth century one is obliged to include the name of Roger Bacon. In an age when to engage in any kind of scientific research was to risk, not only one's professional standing, but even one's life, Roger Bacon went day after day into his little laboratory and carried on his experiments until he was sent to prison, where he remained in solitary confinement for fourteen years; and, thanks originally to him, we of this generation are able to use with almost miraculous effect the so-called scientific method. Any list of the half dozen bravest men of the sixteenth century would certainly include the names of Martin Luther, John Calvin, and John Knox. And such names as Lord Shaftesbury, William Lloyd Garrison, and Leo Tolstoy would certainly appear in any list of the half dozen bravest men of the nineteenth century. The attempt to enlighten the mind of the race, to purify and fortify the heart of the race, to lift to a somewhat higher level the life of the race has always offered, and will continue to offer, abundant opportunity for the display of heroism. During the next quarter century it would, I think, be safe to predict that the very greatest of all opportunities for the display of courage will be offered, not by war, but by the movement to get rid of war.

And when it comes to a cause that is big enough to bind men to men in an indissoluble fellowship, could you think of anything that would serve nearly so well as a gallant attempt to achieve a more noble kind of civilization? The World War revealed the possibility of team work and demonstrated the necessity of it. Until the Allied Forces pooled their resources and placed their military forces under a single command, they suffered one terrible reverse after another. But the World War failed to generate a power that was able permanently to hold people together; and the reason is not far to seek. The motives to which war appeals are chiefly fear and hate, neither of which has proved to be a permanently cohesive force. In the presence of a common danger men may be drawn together by a common fear. In the presence of a diabolically pictured enemy they may be drawn together by a common hate. But after the armistice has been signed what happens? America witnesses the pitiful and sometimes brutal absurdities of a Ku Klux Klan. England witnesses a general strike. Europe is still witnessing a regrettable friction between former allies, the English and the French. War cannot hold people together because it is essentially destructive. The only thing that can hold people permanently together is something creative, the Kingdom of God.

LOSING—FINDING

James I. Vance

"He that findeth his life shall lose it, and he that loseth his life for my sake shall find it."
                                                Matthew x.39

James I. Vance is a man of so many interests and accomplishments that it is difficult to know where to begin in a brief account of his work. One instinctively thinks of such books as his *Young Man Four-Square, Royal Manhood, Rise of a Soul, The Life of Service,* and is inclined to forget that he has been professor of homiletics in Vanderbilt University, served as moderator of the Presbyterian Church in the U. S., as chairman of the executive committee on foreign missions in his Church and as chairman of the Protestant Relief Committee. He was born in Arcadia, Tennessee, in 1862, received both his A.B. and A.M. degrees from King College in the same state. He was graduated from Union Theological Seminary, Virginia, in 1886 and was ordained into the ministry of the Presbyterian Church in the U. S. the same year. Various colleges have conferred upon him honorary degrees. He is a platform speaker of extensive experience and a contributor to magazines and reviews.

Since 1910 Dr. Vance has been pastor of the First Church, Nashville. Other than the books mentioned above, he has written *Simplicity in Life, Young Man's Make-Up, Life's Terminals, The Breaking of the Bread, Being A Preacher, God's Open, Forbid Him Not,* and *Love Trails of the Long Ago.*

LOSING—FINDING

"He that findeth his life shall lose it, and he that loseth his life for my sake shall find it."
Matthew x.39

Of late, many people have been talking of what they have lost. Before that, they were talking of what they had made. Then the world crash in the stock market, and those who had failed to run to cover in time saw their paper profits wiped out over night.

It is worth while to reflect on the fact that there are some values which are not affected when stocks break. There is life. And here is a good verse for those who would capitalize life values. "He that findeth his life shall lose it, and he that loseth his life for my sake shall find it."

I hope that everyone who reads this sermon may find a helpful message in what I am to say. But I am especially anxious that youth may find the sermon helpful. I want to speak more particularly to them, to those who are selecting their vocations, who are just entering on business or professional or industrial tasks, and to all those who are in course of preparation and must soon answer the question of life investment.

Recently I was talking to a friend in an Eastern city whose son is a student in the Pennsylvania State College. The father had just received a letter from the college authorities telling him that his son was not doing very well in his studies. He had managed to creep by in his grades and to pass his examinations, but he was capable of doing better work. The president of the college thought that the boy's father might do something to stir him to better

63

work. The father wrote a letter, and he had just received his son's reply. The young man in this letter admitted that he was doing poorly at college, that his work was below the mark, but he said: "Father, I've been wondering what it's all about. I am rather dazed. The fact is, I have not found myself."

Perhaps there are many young men and women in and out of college to-day who feel somewhat as this youth felt. It would be great to help them find themselves, to say something that would help them to discover what it is all about.

YOUR CAPITAL

One's life is his capital,—not his circumstances. These have their effect, to be sure. Circumstances may help us tremendously in getting started and in keeping going. But circumstances are not our capital.

Neither are heredity, ancestors, forebears. To be sure, good blood and an honorable name and a heritage of decency and respectability are a great blessing. It is something to acquire as one's birthright a certificate that will guarantee an education and a chance.

The age in which we live is not our capital, although this may be a big help. One has a finer chance in the twentieth century than in the tenth, in the modern world than in the dark ages.

One's capital is not his nationality. Some think it better to be born with a white skin than a black, an American citizen than an African. It is great to belong to a nation that places on your tongue a language that will carry your message around the world, rather than inherit the jargon of the jungle for your mother tongue.

The land in which one lives is not his capital. It is a help, to be sure. It is better to live in America than in

Soviet Russia, in England than Mexico, under the Stars and Stripes than under a flag of autocracy and despotism.

But you are your greatest asset,—not your heredity, not your environment, but your personality. Personality is the biggest fact in life.

There are those who lack these things about which I have been speaking, but who by the sheer and matchless might of a resolute and determined will and a courageous personality have reversed the verdict of circumstances, thrown off the handicap of heredity, and won out in the race of life.

Mr. Stryker's life of Andrew Johnson is worth reading. It is a great book. Every American should read it. From plain origin, self-educated, fought bitterly throughout his entire administration as president of the United States by as corrupt and infamous a group of scoundrels as mendacious historians have ever attempted to canonize, tried for impeachment and defeating his enemies by only one vote, standing firmly through all the storm and tumult of those days for the Constitution, President Andrew Johnson will go down in history as one of the greatest presidents of the United States. Mr. Stryker calls his book, "A Study In Courage."

But when all these things are plus and not minus qualities in life's equation, when instead of subtracting from one's personality the disaster of a hostile environment and the drawback of a damaging heredity, one adds what is acquired by good birth and decent surroundings, life would seem to be capitalized to the point of certain and assured success. This is the condition of most of the young people of America. It is the good fortune of the students in the colleges and universities of our land today. They have well-nigh everything in their favor.

The gentleman referred to whose son is a student in

the Pennsylvania State College had to struggle for his education. He faced obstacles to which his son is a stranger. He went to school for a year, and then worked a year to make enough money to go to school again. Down in Haiti the schools the government has organized offer all the advantages of an education free of charge. The students in the Agricultural School recently have struck, and the students in the other schools went on a sympathetic strike, because these agricultural students were not paid a bonus for enjoying the privileges of a free education.

If we cannot to-day get good results out of the fortunate conditions which surround college students, the effort is hopeless. If we find it impossible to grow strong, clean, self-reliant, self-controlled, well-balanced, capable manhood; gentle, refined, unselfish, home-loving, home-making, nation-saving womanhood, out of our schools and colleges of the present day, the outlook is dark and civilization doomed.

But whatever the outside advantages or disadvantages may be, whatever is behind or before, whatever the opportunity may offer or the market present, youth stands a complete human life, with a body more wonderfully fashioned and more marvelously fitted for its task than any machine ever made; with a mind that can think to the farthest limit of space and down into the profoundest problems; with emotions in which mix and mingle all the passions and impulses, all the loves and hates, all the ambitions and aspirations, that have stirred humanity from the dawn of the race; with potentialities that border on godhood, with capacities as big as heaven, with volitions that are dynamic, and with tendencies that are divine. What a piece of work is man—any man, even the most commonplace and mediocre! What a piece of work is man! There is our capital, our incalculable asset. There is our biggest, our only real problem—our life. What are we going to do with it?

DECISION

Each one must decide for himself. Each is the arbiter of his destiny. Others can help, the church can pray, friends can advise, the college can train and equip, parents can counsel; but every individual must decide the question for himself.

We are free. Let no silly metaphysics, no crooked theology, no rotten philosophy, befog the mind on that point. God is sovereign, but one thing He has sovereignly foreordained is human freedom. Therefore, His decree, instead of destroying freedom, is the one thing that forever irrevocably establishes it. If one does not see this, it is because he has not climbed high enough; to see what is on the other side of the mountain, one must stand on the mountain top. Perhaps some day we shall climb high enough to discover that Divine sovereignty and human freedom are in entire harmony.

One's life is in his own hands. It is a tremendous responsibility. He may form habits that enslave him, but the chains cannot be placed on his wrists without his consent. Hypnotism seems to be a mood in which personality is dominated by an outside force. But no man can be hypnotized against his will. No temptation ever overcame any man until he had given his permission. Every habit we form is formed willingly, every indulgence freely.

A man is responsible for himself. He cannot unload his responsibility. He has choice. He possesses will power. Next to omnipotence, will power is the mightiest force that operates in this world. There is a drive about the human will that is well-nigh resistless.

Your will decides what you will do with your life. The choice you make is conclusive. It creates character, controls conduct, shapes tendency, fixes destiny. Here is your life and there is your will. Your will says what you will do with your life.

> "To-day we fashion destiny,
> The web of fate we spin."

MANY ANSWERS

There are many answers given to the question: What shall I do with my life? Some answer with a shrug of the shoulders. They decline to consider the question. They refuse to discuss it. They will drift with the tide. They will let nature take its course. They will leave life's garden to grow as it may, which means an acre of weeds.

Another says: "I will enjoy life. That is what life is for. Let us have a good time. Any price for a new thrill. The pleasure god is the only deity worth worshiping. Down with a religion that taboos happiness!"

Others waste life. Possessing splendid gifts, having superb natural qualities, they allow all to go to waste. Genius is far commoner than is imagined. What is lacking is the application and industry, the sweat and toil, needful to translate genius into success. Many a life starts with brilliant and spectacular promise, but soon the candidate for greatness disappoints his friends and shames himself simply because he permits his great powers to rot out in indolence and disuse.

Still others tax life for the sake of success. The world has something they want, some position, some possession, some kind of power, fame, money, culture, call it what you may. They are willing to wear out and burn up the thing called life in order to reach the goal of their ambition. They are like a ship that ran out of fuel in mid-ocean and burned up its furnishings and supplies to reach port. Such people spoil a life to earn a living.

Some would save their life. They would protect it against disaster, insure it against trouble, guard it from misfortune. Their effort is to keep away from everything that is unpleasant and disagreeable. They build barriers around themselves. They seek exemption. They sigh for immunity. Such life is little more than stagnation.

These are some of the answers given to the greatest of all questions, and there are numbers of people who shape their lives accordingly. They are to be found in all professions and vocations. Whatever they attempt to do in life, they do it with the general purpose of trying to find life. Surely life itself (was meant for something higher, finer, more satisfying, more enriching.

GOD'S PLAN

God has a plan for every life. One may accept or reject His plan, but the plan is there. The better we understand God, the more we discover what He is about, the better we understand ourselves, the more we discover what we are for, the more evident it becomes that God has a plan. He does not work at random. He does not move aimlessly. He matches men and worlds. He relates personality and history. He connects individuals and eras. He does not cast the multitudes of human beings into time's unending stream to sink or swim or drift.

God does not deal in generalities. He is as profoundly interested in the infinitely small as in the infinitely great. The same Divine concern, the same sublime order, manifest themselves in the tiny atom as in the boundless universe. God's plan is all-inclusive. He watches a sparrow's flight; the flare of a comet, and the current of a summer zephyr are as securely steadied by His omnipotence as are the journeys of the cycling stars.

How much more, then, does God's plan cover human life, his loftiest creation? If God has a plan for my life, I should be concerned to know what it is. If when He thought of me first, He thought of what I should be, of where I should go, of what I should do, and of how I should relate myself to my Maker and His world, surely I cannot afford to drift aimlessly and without purpose down the years. It is not enough to be doing something. It is important to be doing the thing for which I was intended.

When God's plan and my life purpose harmonize, my life will be lived to the noblest uses and for the highest ends. Therefore, before life can be capitalized aright, one must ask what God would have him do with his life. He must seek to discover the Divine plan. No one can settle his life vocation aright until he settles it in harmony with the plan of his Maker. This is where men miss their calling. They have ignored God's plan for them. They are not doing the thing He intended them to do.

I was taking lunch with a minister in Pittsburgh. He is one of the ablest of the younger ministers in that city. For six years he had been practicing law. He was not satisfied. Evidently he was not doing the thing he was meant to do. One day he said to a ministerial friend: "What would you think of me if I were to tell you that I was about to give up law and enter the ministry?" His friend replied: "I have often wondered why you did not choose the ministry instead of the law." That night he said to his wife: "How would you feel if I should quit practicing law and become a preacher?" She said: "Nothing could make me happier." He is satisfied now. He knows what it is all about. He has found himself.

Whatever vocation one may enter, God's philosophy for life is the same. He does not tell us to enjoy life, to waste it, to save it. He tells us to lose it. "He that loseth his life for my sake shall find it." It is a strange answer. Yet it is the answer that faces us wherever we turn. It is the answer that sings itself across the harvest fields. How shall a grain of wheat find itself? "Except a grain of wheat fall into the ground and die, it abideth alone." It is the answer that is wafted from all fragrant, blooming gardens. Except roses and lilies and peonies and honeysuckle wither and die, they will never blossom again. It is the answer that comes to us from the life of God Himself. It is the story of the dying Christ on the cross. He came not to please Himself, but to give His life a ransom for many. He said: "And I, if I be lifted up from the earth, will draw all men unto me. This he spake signifying what death he should die." "As he laid down his life for us, so ought we to lay down our lives for the brethren."

However life is to be employed or invested, it can be found only by those who lose it. Service is the secret of greatness. It is not what we do for ourselves, but what we do for others, that counts. As one scans the world's skyline, the great figures that come into view are ever those who serve.

What shall we say of Commander Byrd, that brilliant, gifted, adventurous, high-minded young Virginian? What was he doing amid the Antarctic ice? Was he making a reputation? Was he merely seeking adventure? Was he in quest of fame? Was he grubbing for money? Did he hope his trip would make him a millionaire? We know him too well for that. He has made his purpose plain. He was trying to serve the interests of mankind. Every day he was placing his life in jeopardy. And he is finding life by losing it.

The highest type of service is given by those who go on this great adventure sustained by the motive that sustained Christ. They are losing life to build a better world, to end fear and slay hate, to make men friendly, to usher in human brotherhood, to lift burdens and right wrongs, to make men love one another. This is what He means when He speaks of "losing life for my sake." I wonder if it might not mean for some who are asking "Where?" a life devoted to the Gospel ministry? Perhaps it might send some of our high-minded youth not to the North Pole nor the South Pole, but to some mission field, there to lose life in the greatest of all adventures.

This is what took my dear friend Lewis Lancaster. He has gone back to China. He has gone back to the people who burned his home and tried to kill him. They stood him up to be shot in the Nanking riot. He barely escaped with his life. But he has taken his wife and his children back into the danger zone to take up once more the work of losing life for Christ's sake. A life laid down in this kind of service can never be lost.

Perhaps you have read a wonderful book called "The Splendor of God." It was written by Mrs. Honoré Willsie Morrow. It is the story of Adoniram Judson and his lovely wife Anne, the first missionaries to Burma. It is a story of hardship, suffering, trial, disappointment, peril, death. It is a sad story. But it thrills you from the start. For years they had not a convert, and never many. The children born to them soon died. Anne followed the children. Imprisonment, the vilest surroundings, the harshest treatment that cruelty could devise, every day like a cross, chained for a year and a half to the floor, uncared-for, with just enough food to keep the broken body and the weary soul together,—such was the story. And the novelist calls it "The Splendor of God." It is not until you have turned almost the last page in the book that you divine her meaning. But she is right. The splendor of God is Calvary. It is the life laid down. It is the life that is undying, that can never die.

This is the trail to glory. This is the path along which have passed the great souls who have caught the vision and who have won the cross. This is the Divinity of Him Who came not to be ministered unto, but to minister, and to give His life a ransom for many. It is the glory of Him Who said: "I am among you as one that serveth." And it is the glory of all whose hands and feet bear the marks of kinship with Him.

> "They climbed the steep ascent of heaven
> Through peril, toil, and pain;
> O, God, to us may grace be given
> To follow in their train."

TALKING PEACE AND THINKING WAR

Charles E. Jefferson

> *"They have healed the hurt of my people slightly, saying, Peace, Peace; when there is no peace."*
>
> *Jeremiah vi.14*

The retirement of Charles E. Jefferson from the pastorate of Broadway Tabernacle on his seventieth birthday brought to a close one of the most notable careers in the history of the Protestant Church in America. Dr. Jefferson said in offering his resignation: "For over thirty years I have said that I should rather be the pastor of the Broadway Tabernacle in New York City than hold any other position on earth. It is not often granted to a man to possess through so long a period the one thing which if he were given a choice of all the world's prizes he would choose first. Such has been my happy lot." In a ballot several years ago 25,000 ministers of every denomination included Dr. Jefferson on the list of the twenty-five most influential preachers in America.

Following his graduation from Ohio Wesleyan in 1882, he became superintendent of public schools in Worthington, Ohio, going from there to Boston University for the study of law. In Boston he came under the influence of Phillips Brooks and decided to enter the ministry. He was graduated from the Boston University School of Theology in 1887 with the degree of S.T.B. He served the Chelsea Congregational Church, Chelsea, Mass., until 1898, when he came to Broadway Tabernacle. Many universities, including Yale, have conferred honorary degrees upon him. He is the author of more than a score of books, perhaps the most notable being his *The Character of Jesus, The Minister as a Shepherd* and *The Character of Paul.* From the first he has been an indefatigable worker in the cause of peace.

TALKING PEACE AND THINKING WAR

*"They have healed the hurt of my people slightly,
saying, Peace, Peace; when there is no peace."*
Jeremiah vi.14

Who said that? Jeremiah was sure God said it. These words he dares to put into the mouth of God. Of whom is God speaking? The prophets and priests of Israel, the anointed leaders of the Church, the ordained teachers of religion, the official spiritual guides of the nation. It is they who have healed the hurt of God's people slightly. They have been worthless surgeons. They have not examined the wound carefully nor probed it thoroughly. They have not gone deep enough. They have not found out how dangerous the wound is. They have spoken smooth words to make everybody feel comfortable. With beautiful phrases they have covered over ugly facts. The nation is sick and they have made light of its illness. They have said "Peace, peace," when there is no peace. Our theme today is Talking Peace and Thinking War.

This is the eighteenth day of May, the thirty-first anniversary of the opening of the First Hague Peace Conference. That conference was called in the year 1899 by the Czar of Russia. That is a great date in the history of the world. For a generation that event has been celebrated every year by groups of peace lovers in various quarters of the Christian world. Since the world war the Churches have for the most part made Armistice Day the day for the annual peace celebration, the eighteenth day of May being turned over to the instruction of boys and girls in

77

the duty and grace of international good will. It is fitting this year that a peace sermon should be preached in the month of May in all our Churches because the recent Naval Conference in London is uppermost in all our minds. Now is a good time to take a survey of the world situation and to appraise the significance of the conference which has just recently adjourned.

The purpose of this sermon is to clarify our minds in regard to the achievements of this conference and to call attention to certain revelations which the conference has made. Many persons are at present perplexed in regard to the outcome of the conference. Some think it a failure, while others think it a success. I presume we all have practically the same experience when we come to grapple with intricate problems which stir up controversy. We find it difficult to ascertain the facts and we find it still more difficult to arrive at satisfying conclusions. There are so many papers and magazines and books, each one telling us a different story, there are so many reporters and editors and interpreters and commentators and experts and they present us such clashing opinions that we find ourselves wandering in a fog. The most of us have little time for reading and still less time for thinking, and all we can do is to snatch up the odds and ends of other men's opinions, leaving us at last with no definite convictions of our own. It is fitting that in the House of Prayer we should on the Lord's Day think carefully and reverently about one of the outstanding events of our generation.

Let us begin with the question, what did the conference fail to do? It was called for the purpose of securing a five-power treaty on reduction in naval armaments. It failed to secure a five-power treaty. The aim was to induce the United States and Great Britain and France and Italy and Japan to put their names to a treaty which would reduce the naval equipment of these five nations. Such a treaty was not signed. The most which could be achieved was a three-power treaty. In Washington in 1922, a five-power treaty was signed. That was considered almost a miracle but the miracle could not be repeated. The delegates to the conference had to be content with a treaty signed only by the United States and Great Britain and Japan. This was a disappointment.

The second disappointment was the failure of the conference to reduce cruiser tonnage. The conference at Washington City had restricted the building of battleships but no agreement could be reached in regard to cruisers. One reason why the London Conference was called was to work out the problem of cruisers. But alas, the London Conference did not reduce the tonnage of cruisers. On the contrary it increased it. It gave us the privilege of building more cruisers. Already a bill has been introduced in our House of Representatives calling for the expenditure of nearly one billion dollars on new ships.

The third failure of the conference was the failure to reduce the number of aircraft carriers. It had been hoped that the figure agreed on in Washington in 1922 might be reduced. But to reduce it was found impossible. The Washington figure still stands.

The conference failed to enter upon a course looking for the complete abolition of the battleship. Great Britain wanted to do this, so also did Italy. We objected and so it was not done.

The conference refused to abolish the submarine. We were ready to do it, so also was Great Britain, but France objected and so also did Japan. We are still to be plagued by the submarine.

These were the five failures of the conference. Because of these failures many are ready to pronounce the conference a complete failure. There is a strong tide of skepticism now flowing across the world. Here and there one hears a gush of cynical laughter. The cynics are all saying, "I told you so. You never can get anywhere by disarmament conferences. The nations have always fought and they will fight to the last day." Others more radical declare that the conference did harm. The situation is now worse than it was. New complications have been created and bad feelings have been aroused which it will take a generation to recover from. The voice of pessimism is now heard in many lands.

But while the conference did not accomplish all that had been hoped for, there were several things attained which should not be overlooked. In the first place the conference extended what is called the naval holiday. This means a period in which no additional battleships can be built. By the Washington Conference this period was made ten years. Since the Washington Conference not a new battleship has been built by any of the five nations participating in that conference. This time has now been extended five years. It is not a long extension but it is encouraging.

The conference reduced the battleships of the three contracting nations by nine. Nine capital ships are to be scrapped. The fleets are to be reduced to the extent of 230,000 tons. It is not much but it is something.

The conference reduced the submarine tonnage. The reduction is not great but it is not to be despised.

The conference reduced the tonnage of destroyers. Here again the reduction is slight but though slight it is a cause for thanksgiving.

The fifth achievement of the conference was in the

world of the spirit. This conference helped to establish more firmly the habit of nations to gather around a table for the discussion of international affairs. It is a good habit and the oftener it is practiced the better it will be for mankind. Representatives of five great nations cannot come together for ninety days and talk over matters of common concern without forming friendships which will endure as long as life lasts. It is impossible for able and noble men to meet face to face and converse with one another for three months without a widening of the mind and a broadening of the heart. No man returned from that conference without an heightened estimate of the people of the other nations with which he had been dealing. There is a better understanding now than there was before the conference met and the fact that this conference was held will only prepare the way for another. We are forming the habit of conferring on our problems of international conduct and the London Conference was only one in a long series of conferences which are certain to be held.

And so our Secretary of State, Mr. Stimson, is justified I think in his optimism. He told the boys and girls of this country over the radio the other day that the conference was a long step toward world peace. If you wonder how he could make a statement so cheery you must remember that he understands the situation better than we do. He knows the obstacles to be grappled with, and the difficulties to be conquered, and the tremendous forces working against world peace which must be combatted and overcome, and so he feels that any advance however slight is to be reckoned a glorious success. He sees that the path to peace is "a series of successive steps" and he rejoices that another step in the series has been taken. There is only one word in his statement which I should care to change and that is the word "long." A step has indeed been taken but it is hardly a long step. And yet though short it is not to be sneered at. It was a step upward and a step upward must of necessity be short. When one is climbing a mountain and especially when he is climbing the mountain of God, a step cannot be long, but a short step upward counts for more than a longer step on the level. We are no doubt higher than we were.

The London Conference was a great illumination. It revealed as by a flash of lightning two facts which we ought to ponder. It showed us the limitations of the power of our political officials. We talk about our "rulers" and are often misled by the sound of the word "ruler." We assume that they are dictators, whereas they are only our servants. They can do only what the people permit them to do. The world is in the grip of Democracy, and in a democracy it is public opinion which determines what can be done. When the London Conference was called, conditions seemed well nigh perfect. We have a President who is a Quaker. He is a sincere lover of peace. He works always in favor of peace. He was not content with a limitation of armaments, he wanted a reduction in armaments. His most emphatic word was "reduction." But Mr. Hoover is not a stronger friend of peace than is the Prime Minister of Great Britain, Mr. Ramsay MacDonald. He has for years been one of the outstanding peace workers of the world. He is ready at all times to make large sacrifices for peace. It was he and Mr. Hoover who created the London Conference. One other man ought to be added, Monsieur Briand. In devotion to peace no man can be placed above this illustrious Frenchman. He is one of the greatest men now alive. With him the love of peace is a passion. He burns with fervent heat. These three men more than any others were responsible for calling the

London Conference. They created an atmosphere in which it seemed inevitable that the conference should prove a success. The delegations sent to the conference were made up of able and noble men, men who believe in peace and are willing to work hard to obtain it. Our own delegation was one of which every American had reason to be proud. All seven members were men of great ability and wide experience and high ideals. It would have been difficult to select a group of seven Americans superior in calibre and nobility and devotion to peace than the seven men who were sent to London. Our delegation was matched by delegations equally able and loyal from the other four countries. The situation seemed to be ideal for securing the desired results. But how little was accomplished compared with what had been dreamed. These delegations had to keep their eye on the governments behind them. Our rulers cannot do what they please or secure all the results which they desire. We know that our own President finds himself balked again and again. He is said to have more power than any other ruler in the world but his power is held rigorously in check. The United States Senate can thwart him whenever it so desires. In determining foreign policy he and the Senate have coordinate authority, and no treaty can be signed to which the Senate refuses to give its assent. It was necessary therefore for our delegation to keep its eye on the Senate. It had to watch its step. It could not submit a treaty which the Senate would be sure to reject. Our delegation therefore had to move slowly. The same situation exists in all these five countries except Italy. They are all under the sway of the democratic principle. They have government by the people. England is a democracy, a democracy in a more flexible form than our own. We cannot get rid of a cabinet which we do not like in less than four years, whereas England can get rid of an unpopular cabinet in a night. The position of Mr. Ramsay MacDonald is exceedingly precarious, and he may be thrown out of office any day. It was necessary for the British delegation therefore to keep its eye on the House of Commons, and consequently no long step could be taken. In France the form of government lends itself to swift action. Cabinets can be thrown out with amazing celerity. Monsieur Tardieu and his co-workers had to keep their eyes all the time on the French Parliament, for no treaty would be acceptable which went an inch too far. This then, was the situation. Every delegation had to keep its eye on its government, and every government had to keep its eye on the people. Without the consent of the people nothing of importance can be accomplished. This brings us face to face with the size of our problem. The people must be educated to think peace. It is a big job, a long job and it will not be completed in our generation. All the nations must be educated. It is not sufficient to educate one only. No nation will walk ahead alone. They will move all together or they will not advance at all. America must be educated, so must Great Britain, so must France, so must Italy, and so must Japan. It is a herculean task and to achieve it will require the energetic and indefatigable labor of many years. The wound is deep and it cannot be healed in a day.

A second fact emerged from the conference. We saw with appalling vividness how difficult it is to change the thought habits of men. It is comparatively easy to change the phrases on men's lips, it is well nigh impossible to change the habits of their thinking. Thirty-one years ago the word "peace" was scarcely heard outside of limited and isolated circles. There were at that time groups of earnest people ardently devoted to the cause of peace but they were by the majority considered fanatics, impractical dreamers, crying for the moon. The word "peace" was spoken often apologetically, sometimes derisively. The word "war" was spoken everywhere and usually with pride. Men said that war is a school of virtue, that it is necessary to keep sharp the fighting edge, that a little blood-letting does a nation good. But since the world war all that has changed. The word "peace" has forged to the front. It is now in every mouth. You cannot open a magazine or paper that your eye does not fall upon that word. Everybody now believes in peace and wants it. Everybody talks about it. Everybody abhors war. The generals and rear admirals are all peace advocates. They take their place among the pacifists in deprecating war.

But it is possible to talk peace and think war. That is what the world is just now doing. That is what the Naval Conference did. It was called in the interest of peace. Its purpose was to safeguard the peace of the world. The nations which went into it had all signed the Pact of Paris. The Pact of Paris is this: "The High Contracting Parties solemnly declare in the names of their respective peoples that they condemn recourse to war for the solution of international controversies, and renounce it as an instrument of national policy in their relations with one another." The United States signed that, so did Great Britain and so did France and so did Italy and so did Japan. They also signed this: "The High Contracting Parties agree that the settlement or solution of all disputes or conflicts of whatever nature or of whatever origin they may be, which may arise among them, shall never be sought except by pacifist means." All the five nations pledged themselves to that.

All the five nations had talked peace, but as soon as

they came together they showed that they were all thinking war. They had renounced war on paper, but they had
not renounced it in their hearts. They were still thinking
war. They all with one accord thought war. And so the
cardinal subject of discussion was parity. This is a Latin
word which means equality. Equality is also a Latin word.
We grew weary of the word "equality" and took up the
shorter word "parity." The air in London was vibrant
with that word. Parity was the supreme end aimed at.
Parity in what? In peace? No, not in peace. Parity in
war. Not parity in generosity, in trustfulness, in sympathy, or in mutual helpfulness, or in good will, but parity
in the instruments of war. The nations had renounced
war but they spent all their time in measuring and com-
paring the instruments of war. They had pledged themselves never to seek the solution of any dispute of any
kind except by pacific means, but they went to work at
once to balance gun with gun and ton with ton, assuming
that all of them would some day fight and that every
nation must be prepared. It would be ludicrous if it were
not so tragic. It would be laughable if it were not so heart-
breaking. What must God think of a world like this, a
world in which sensible and honorable men talk peace and
think war? Parity in war was the *summum bonum* on
which every delegation had set its heart. Parity was the
devil which made havoc of the conference, and almost
completely wrecked it. Delegations were ready to risk
smashing the conference and even wrecking civilization
rather than give up their demand for parity. A prophet
long ago represented God as saying to a foolish nation,
"You worship Me with your mouth but your heart is far
from Me." The London Conference has shown us more
clearly than ever that the world's wound is deep and that
it cannot be healed slightly.

The conference is over, and now what shall we do? Let me suggest two bits of advice. First of all watch! Keep your eyes open. Pay attention to the agencies which work day and night to train men to think war. It is the habit of thinking war which must be broken. Until that habit is weakened no naval conference can prosper. The War Department and the Navy Department of our Government work without ceasing to train our people to think war. The brigadier-generals and rear admirals are popular guests at banquets. They always sit at the head of the table and what they say invariably gets first page publicity. It is amazing how frequently these men speak and how zealous they are—even after they are retired—to train the nation to think war. And they are prolific writers also. Their literary output is immense, and they all write with but one object in view, the training of peaple to think war. The army and navy play war games. They play them every year. They play them in the eyes of the public. They used to play them on land and sea and now they play them also in the air. The games are spectacular. They are sometimes thrilling. They are played for the purpose of training us to think war. Every game played demonstrates our need of stronger defense. Only recently we have had warnings written on the sky, calling our attention to our defenceless condition. We have been given a new lesson in the art of thinking war.

Every year the navy is put on exhibition. It is truly an imposing spectacle. It costs hundreds of millions of dollars and why should it not be shown off? It is ours, why should we not enjoy it? The Hudson River furnishes a magnificent stage, and six million people are eager to enjoy the exhibition. The display is beautiful in the day but even more beautiful at night. The playing of the searchlights on the city is dramatic and entrancing. That is an excellent way of educating a whole city to think war. The lights are bright and we gaze on them with the *naïveté* of little children. A child always likes something bright. You can amuse it for a long time by dangling bright objects before its eyes. So does the navy dangle its illuminated battleships before us, and paint the heavens with streams of light in order to educate us in thinking war.

And all this gets into the papers. It is not only the people at the mouth of the Hudson who need to be educated but the people on the banks of the Mississippi and on the prairies of the Far West. As a nation we must be educated to think war, and to this work the newspapers give glad and powerful assistance. The Sunday papers take delight in spreading before the nation pictures of the war vessels and of their officers, of the airplanes and of their latest stunts. No such publicity is given to any other branch of the government. The nation is systematically and continuously and effectively trained to think war. No wonder the navy appropriations remain high. We spend more money every year on our army and navy than any other nation under heaven. Only a few days ago the House of Representatives passed the Navy Supply Bill for 1931—a bill of $382,000,000. It has often been noted that by a singular coincidence the navy is put on exhibition and the newspapers work overtime with their pictures in the very month in which Congress is discussing the naval appropriations.

But this is only a part of the war-thinking educational program. There must be military training in our schools. It is already established in many of our colleges and the War Department is insistent that it shall go into our high schools. In certain quarters there is pressure to bring it even into our grammar schools. This would be ideal, to have all the high school boys and all the grammar school boys of America trained to think war. We could then have even higher army and navy budgets!

Another feature of the educational program is the summer military training camps. The War Department is proud of the progress it is making. It reports that this coming summer there will be 226,000 boys in these camps. All these boys will be trained to think war. Many persons see no harm whatever in this military drill. They are impressed by the plausible argument that it is a good thing to keep boys in the open air, and to train them to stand erect and to give them elementary lessons in obedience, and to bring them under discipline. Surely all these things are good, and it would seem that only a fanatic could have any objection to them. But those who speak thus overlook an important fact. The most far-reaching and momentous thing done in these summer camps is the training of our boys to think war. These 226,000 boys have 226,000 fathers and 226,000 mothers, and these parents are also being trained to think war. Nearly every boy has a sweetheart, and therefore 226,000 girls are being trained to think war. The future mothers of the country are being trained to think war. Every boy in camp has grandfathers and grandmothers and uncles and aunts and companions and friends and all these are being trained to think war. But these 226,000 boys are not the only ones to be drilled this summer. There are 7,463 of the R.O.T.C. and 17,190 in the Officers' Reserve, and 57,000 of the C.M.T.C. and 163,780 of the National Guard. Here are an additional host of a quarter of a million men all being trained to think war, and around every one of these men are concentric circles of men and women more or less influenced by the man at the center. Several millions of Americans are being trained by the

War Department to think war. So long as we think war the army and navy appropriations will never go down, and the way of the peace conference will continue to be hard.

And therefore we must educate. We must plant the seed of peace. We must plant it in the hearts of our young people in our colleges, and in the hearts of our boys and girls in all the high schools and in all the grammar schools, and in all the primary schools, and in all the kinder-gartens, and in all the homes. We are not going to win the cause of peace by any methods which are spectacular or any measures which make a noise. The work must be done quietly and continuously and enthusiastically, certain that the harvest will at last be great. It is not by thunder or by lightning but by the still small voice of mothers and teachers that the world will at last come to think peace.

Let us not then be deceived by the superficial talk of those who imagine that because men use the word "peace" the curse of war has been abolished. The wound is deep. The root of the trouble is in the heart. Many persons think the problem is an economic one. It may be in part but it is primarily a religious one. If the problem is ever settled it will be settled by the Christian Church. Christian men and women must face this problem and never allow their eyes to wander away from it. If we are indeed the followers of the Prince of Peace then we must work for peace and make sacrifices for it. A preacher is never nearer to the center of the Gospel than when he is urging men to think peace and he is never more faithful to his mission as an ambassador of the Son of God than when he is exhorting men to work with their might against the genius and schemes of those who in blindness are endeavoring to perpetrate the reign of Caesar.

The root of the trouble is spiritual. It is suspicion which paralyzed the London Conference. The nations do not trust one another. All five nations signed the Pact of Paris, but no one of them believed that the others would keep their word. We did not trust Great Britain, nor did Great Britain trust us, France did not trust Italy and Italy did not trust France, none of them trusted Japan and Japan is distrustful of us all. It was the demon of suspicion which made all the nations afraid. They are afraid of one another and that is why they feel they must walk encased in armor.

It is because of our fear that we cannot come together. The wound is deep. Only God can heal it. Only God in Christ can heal it. Only God in Christ on the cross. What does that mean? Only sacrificial love can heal it. The cross was not visible in the London Conference. There was no thought of sacrificial love. Christ was not lifted up. But an idol was set up—an idol called Parity—and the nations bowed down before it!

IMMORTALITY

John A. W. Haas

"God is not the God of the dead, but of the living."
Matthew xxii.32

Since 1904 John A. W. Haas has been president and professor of philosophy at Muhlenberg College. Prior to that time he was pastor of St. Paul's Lutheran Church, New York City, and has been throughout his active career one of the outstanding leaders of Lutheran forces in America. He received his A.B., A.M., and B.D. degrees from the University of Pennsylvania and in 1914 that University conferred upon him the degree of Doctor of Laws. Following his work in the Lutheran Theological Seminary, he spent two years (1887-88) in the University of Leipzig.

Besides a number of pamphlets and brochures on religious topics, Dr. Haas is the author of the following books: *Trends of Thought and Christian Truth, In the Light of Faith, Freedom and Christian Conduct, The Unity of Faith and Knowledge, The Truth of Faith.* He is a contributor to religious periodicals and a frequent speaker before ministerial gatherings and social organizations.

IMMORTALITY

In the restlessness of our day with its religious uncertainty, and its doubt about many great spiritual truths, among certain intellectual groups, many convictions of faith are in the flux. Truths which were never denied in the Deistic controversies, such as the existence of a personal God, the immortality of the soul, and the freedom of the will, are today set aside widely. The ever living soul, a belief which earliest mankind found in the realm of dreams, and in the breath of man as in the blowing wind, is denied. The age old tradition of ancient Egyptian religion, and the secrets of Orphism, are treated as negligible. The Christian certainty of life everlasting is thrown on the scrapheap.

There are two outstanding conceptions which militate against man's immortality. The first is the individualistic idea with its bold assertions. Self-conscious men affirm, that they have no desire for immortality, and that they feel no need of it. They make their own thought, derived from unproven or stunted feeling, the judge of a spiritual truth. Regardless of the fact are they, that most men do desire the continuity in eternity of their personality. No life is so complete, and no personality has reached such a possibility of life, attainment, and character, that they are really fulfilled in the accident of death. Universal humanity desires immortality even though some individuals are strongly abnormal. Those who do not want life

95

eternal are exceptions, for as a rule we all desire the permanence of personality for ourselves and our dear ones.

The second idea which opposes man's immortality as a person explains the philosophy of the individualistic want of desire for life eternal. Those who say that they have no longing for eternal continuity, have a thoroughly material view of man. For them he is the mere resultant of the processes of physical nature. He is an integration and a focal unit of the forces of an evolving universe. Human life is mere organic functioning, and man is a collection of behaviorisms. His mind is physiologically conditioned, and he is finally only a higher animal without soul or spirit. Glands make character. There is no evidence of spiritual unity in man. Personality is a complex resulting from actions. It can fall apart so that a man is several personalities at different times. In the light of such science there can be neither soul nor spirit.

But faith is not discomfited by these and like contentions. It has a definite certainty of religious truth and experience rich in reality. Christian belief cannot surrender the soul and its eternal life without denying God. God and the soul stand and fall together. A real soul demands a personal God, and a personal God guarantees a living soul. God is only the God of the living. In Him there is no place for the dead. The approach of faith to the living soul is through the living God.

A LIVING SOUL THROUGH THE LIVING GOD

I. Through the living God as spirit.
II. Through the living God of spirits.
III. Through the living God in Christ.

I. "God is a spirit" is a fundamental Christian conviction. We Christians cannot have any other or lower thought of God. But spirit is not an impersonal or abstract idea under which we classify God. Spirit is personal reality even if some thinkers deal with spirit apart from its concrete existence in personality, as scientists conceive of matter separate from its actual occurrence in diverse forces. The believer is no such speculator. Faith rests on the experienced reality of spirit in personalities. No symbolic abstraction deludes the Christian. He lives in realizable realities of the spirit. For him God cannot be the universe, the great totality, the creative force, the developing world, or any such speculative dream.

It is no illusion of the mind, and no projection of a wish, to which the believer attaches the name of God. God is the eternal Father with whom the Christian communes. He receives again and again a realizing sense of God. By his spirit he perceives the presence of God. In prayer the Christian does not create an ideal of the imagination. He has real contact of living communion. Under God's keeping providence and love life goes on. God is not dead, and He does not die as false prophets announce. He is the everliving and everlasting Father. We have this assurance not by tradition, nor mere hearsay, but by living experience. How can those who have shut themselves out from this experience deny its possibility, or explain it as an hallucination. It is never just to tell men that they have not experienced, and cannot experience, what they definitely know that they have experienced.

Some men can never be sure of their soul because they only know God as an inference or hypothesis. We cannot really find God, our Father, through the evidence of nature. The forces of the universe, or ultimate power, the order of the universe as wisdom, and the demand for a first cause or ground of the world—none of these can lead us farther than philosophic probability. The course of history, and the progress of mankind, do not clearly reveal God, even if they show a power making for righteousness not ourselves. God as living and eternal personality is not found by any such process of reasoning. What reason establishes reason can destroy. God is a necessity of the soul. He is the answer to its cry and the proof of its reality. We must always begin to find ourselves as souls by finding God.

Life as we know it in the world about us is subject to many changes, and it appears in many forms. But these forms die though they hand on life. Our material experiences give no clue to unending life in concrete existences. We touch life as it streams on, but we do not know from nature whence it comes and whither it goes. It is not possible to build up our experiences of natural life into a tower reaching into the heavens and touching God. No material form guaranteed our eternal spirit. Therefore those who live in nature alone can never find the living God nor the living soul.

There is a direct communication of God with man. God comes through His personal revelation, for of Him testify prophets and apostles. These He uses to awaken in us the memory of His image. We do not attain unto God merely by searching our soul. He is not so imprinted upon us that we can know Him without His sending down to us His light and His truth through those to whom He grants a direct vision of Himself. Our faith in God as a personal, eternal spirit comes to us objectively and historically. But we confirm the revealed messages, not merely in the satisfactory answer they give us in our searching after God, but we also know God in our personal contacts with Him, as the God who is from everlasting to everlasting. He is our firm and lasting foundation in the flux of things. The certainty of His endless life, the fact that He is alpha and omega, is with us in and through all our adoration and worship.

II. God is apprehended not only as spirit in Himself, but He is also the Father of all spirits. The certainty of our soul and spirit rests on Him. When Jesus replied to the quibbling query of the Sadducees He asserted, that life everlasting was implied when God allowed Himself to be called the God of Abraham, Isaac, and Jacob. The Ancient of Days made no covenant with those that would die. When He entered into relation with the patriarchs of old He established a permanent bond between Himself and them. The party of the first part, God, in His descent of grace had given endless life to the patriarchs, the party of the second part. He ever was and remains the God of the living, and those with whom He deals cannot die. His power of life is given to His own.

Back of the covenant assurance of God, that the personalities who are His cannot die, lies the creative power of God. He does not project His power and might into a world of matter alone. Out of His own spirit He gives spirit to man. His breath is breathed into man. It is true that in his body man is earth of earth, and that he is tied up with all nature below him. But man is more than body. He is even more than mind which the psychologist analyzes. There is in man the mystery of the spirit. And this mystery is parallel to the mystery of matter and energy. But the reality of our spirits, and the actuality of our souls, lies closer to us than all bodily life. We can never go far outside of our inner selves. It is impossible to unclothe ourselves of our personality. Analyse it as we will it still is there, though in its depths hidden and mysterious. We are our deepest selves, and yet we are more than ourselves. The impress of God is upon us. We are spirits of His spirit, and children of His image. Without such knowledge and faith we are sad and forlorn creatures. But we can find the meaning of our souls only through the same faith by which we apprehend God.

Our souls are not projected into existence by God and then left to themselves. Whether we seek God or whether we try to escape Him, His creative power of spirit sustains our souls and spirits. With all self-will and through all doubt we cannot somehow destroy the divine power that keeps our spirits alive. This truth was forecast by Plato when he argued, that rust might destroy iron, but evil could not destroy our souls. The peculiarity of the life of the spirit is that it does not decay. But men can kill truth and righteousness within themselves, and they may be dead to every good thought and impulse. God may be shut out of human lives by sin, and yet the soul as such does not cease to exist. Whatever final destiny men make for themselves they cannot actually kill the spirit. It is this permanence of the spirit which characterizes it as unique in distinction from the present body. Spirit by its very nature is immortal.

We feel in our deepest longings, which we can only ruthlessly suppress, that our ultimate destiny lies beyond time. The changes and vicissitudes of time do not satisfy us. We do not want to age and grow old. The hope of lasting youth lies close to our hearts. Somehow even bodily death seems strange and sad. But we as we have hope do not surrender our spirits to death. We hear the incessant comfort: "Ye shall not die." It is through the spirit and soul that we cling to life and do not surrender it, for often we grow very tired of our wasting bodies. God has planted the undying faith in the life of the spirit in our souls. We must only be ready to listen to the still, small voice, and not permit the noises and the turmoil of time to silence the whisper of the spirit. God is ever close to us in our inmost life.

God as love must keep our spirits living. Divine love is not like human affection. Human love may cease or die. But even human love at its best is immortal. In its noblest exhibition human love ever lives on. But the love of God wherewith He loves us is without end. Nothing can separate us from this love, neither life nor death. It keeps us and upholds us. It is a denial of the gracious and abundant love of God for us to believe for a moment, that He can permit us to cease as living spirits. He never departs from us, and He never leaves us. The assurance and guarantee of the endless life of the spirit is given us as soon and as long as we accept and dwell within the love of God. His love is ever new and ever life-giving, and in it our souls are hid in all eternity.

III. The final confirmation of the continuance of personality comes to us through the living God in Christ Jesus. It is Christ who by teaching and life has brought to us the knowledge and reality of the living God as our Heavenly Father. We have objective and historical evidence for God in and through Christ, who is the true revealer of the Father. Whosoever seeth and knoweth Christ seeth and knoweth God. In all of Christ's messages life eternal is assumed and often testified to. In the word which corrects the error of the Sadducees who doubted immortality Christ only confirmed all that He said and did. He is never in doubt, but says: "I live and ye shall live also." He promises life abundant and lasting. This is eternal life that we might know now and always God and Christ whom He sent.

In the prevalent and constant teaching of Christ on the Kingdom of God the view goes far beyond all time. While the Kingdom has come and is coming now in time as we pray, and while it is the permeating leaven, the great tree growing from the minute mustard seed, the hidden treasure in the field, and the precious pearl to be sought now, nevertheless the Kingdom is not completed and fulfilled in all the ages of time. At the end of history the tares among the wheat of the Kingdom will be removed. The bad fish caught with the good in the gospel net will be cast away. The full glory of the Kingdom lies in the future of eternity. Then will God's realm and rule prevail without let or hindrance as men will do God's will as it is now done in heaven. As the Kingdom includes the souls and spirits of men they must live on in the Kingdom to come. Were men ultimately to die there could be no Kingdom, for the King alone cannot constitute the Kingdom. If we believe Christ's teaching of the Kingdom in all its phases, in its present and in its eternal future, we must accept the fact of immortality for the children of men.

What is implied in the saviorhood of Christ? What is the salvation which He wrought and offers to us? It is truly a present ransom, and it comes now in time to free us from sin and its guilt through the gift of the forgiveness of sins. But does it cease in and with time? Are we saved only in this life and for this present life? The salvation which begins now is the inception of eternal life. Christ redeems us that we might have life everlasting. The endless life is the outcome of salvation. If we disbelieve immortality we must reject the full value of salvation. But if salvation is an experienced reality, as it is for the believer, it carries with it the glorious promise and unending hope of a life, which will far surpass our highest expectations. It does not yet appear what we shall be, but what eye hath not seen, and ear hath not heard, God has prepared for them that love Him.

Immortality has its real historical evidence and its objective basis in the resurrection of Jesus Christ. If we believe His resurrection to have occurred actually we cannot doubt His promise: "I am the resurrection and the life; he that believeth in me, though he were dead, yet shall he live." Wherever men only accept the historic testimony, that the disciples believed that Jesus rose from the dead, and leave His actual resurrection in doubt, they knock out the underpinning of the faith in life eternal. But the witness of the gospel must be rejected, its truthfulness impugned, and the disciples be accused either as impostors, or as men enmeshed in an illusion, if the real resurrection of Jesus is rejected. All Christianity would rest on a lie or deception. But such inferences are impossible to a sane and impartial mind in the face of the historical record. Only a prejudiced opposition to the supernatural can doubt the resurrection of Jesus. Its historic certainty is the believer's rock of ages.

The future life which the Christian hopes for is not only the continuity of the soul. It is the life of the whole human personality, body and soul. Christ brought His body back out of the grave. We too shall not be without a body at the last day, and appear as bare unclothed souls. The old, weak, natural body will decay. But we shall have a spiritual body, a body spirit-filled, spirit-permeated, and spirit-controlled, but still a body though no longer earthly. From weakness our bodies will pass to strength, from mortality to immortality, from natural to spiritual being, and from the taint of sin to glory. We do not consider the body in its ultimate destiny a prison-house of the soul, for even now it is the temple of the eternal Holy Spirit. Christian faith goes beyond the pagan belief in a mere immortality of the soul. It holds and confesses the life of full human personality in body and soul. We shall never be angels, mere spirits, but in all eternity glorified human beings, after the image, and through the power of the eternally glorified body of the Son of Man, in which with His deity, He reigns and lives forever and ever. Amen.

THE PRACTICAL VALUE OF RELIGION

William Pierson Merrill

> "They that wait upon the Lord shall renew
> their strength; they shall mount up with wings
> as eagles; they shall run and not be weary; and
> they shall walk and not faint."
>
> Isaiah xl.31

Few men have been more intelligently active in the cause of international brotherhood and its achievement through the religion of Jesus than has William Pierson Merrill. Since 1915 he has been president of the trustees of the Church Peace Union and tireless in his efforts to give religion that practical value which he speaks of in this sermon. Dr. Merrill is a graduate of Rutgers College, receiving his A.B. in 1887 and his A.M. in 1890. The same year he was ordained a Presbyterian minister. From 1895 to 1911 he was pastor of the Sixth Church, Chicago, and since 1911 has been minister of the historic Brick Church on Fifth Avenue, New York. His concern with the administrative and practical side of Christianity has never lessened his emphasis upon the devotional aspect of his ministry.

His first book, *Faith Building,* appeared in 1885. It was followed in 1900 by *Faith and Sight,* and in 1915 by *Footings For Faith.* Since that time he has published *Christian Internationalism, The Common Creed of Christians, The Freedom of the Preacher,* and *Liberal Christianity.*

THE PRACTICAL VALUE OF RELIGION

*"They that wait upon the Lord shall renew
their strength; they shall mount up with wings
as eagles; they shall run and not be weary; and
they shall walk and not faint."*

Isaiah xl.31

The present age has a keen eye for practical values.
And this is particularly true of the country and city in
which we live.

I am not echoing the easy accusation that America in
general and New York City in particular are materialistic.
There are materialists among us; and, like the two frogs
in the pond, they make so much noise that we think there
are millions of them. But on the whole the people of this
country and city are idealistic. They are not the less
dreamers of dreams that they make their dreams take
solid shape when they wake up.

But life is swift and short, and rich in opportunity.
And we feel very sure that we have no time or strength
to give to that which hasn't practical value.

In such an age it must cause serious concern to anyone
who believes in the vital importance of religion that so
many people let the practice of religion go as a negligible
affair. They say they have no time for it. But if they
honestly thought it had real value, they would find time
for it. People will always take time for what they know
to be vital.

Doubtless the church is to blame in large part for the
fact that so many thoughtful people count the practice
of religion negligible. We ought to be able to set forth

the beauty and worth of our religion in such ways that men would feel they could not do without it, and would look on our churches not as antiquarian curiosities, but as centers of throbbing reality. I know that other ministers feel the burden of this as I do, seldom entering the pulpit without the quick and painful thought, "There must be something that could be said, something that could be done, here in our worship and preaching, that would make the need of God and the glory of God so clear that men could not keep away. O God, *what is it?* Show us what to do and say."

But not all the responsibility rests on the church. Grant the utmost that can be truthfully said of the inadequacy of our worship and preaching, and still it is true that the practice of religion, just as it is, with all its defects, has values no one can afford to miss.

What are they? The text shows. "They that wait upon the Lord shall renew their strength." Is not that a practical value? Life makes terrific demands on us. Anything that will really renew our strength, refresh our energies, increase our capacity to face life with courage, is worth while. That is what the practice of religion will do for us. Any one can prove it by a personal test.

The text goes on to specify. "They shall mount up with wings as eagles. They shall run and not be weary. They shall walk and not faint." Putting that in terms of plain spiritual experience, it means that from the definite practice of religion one can gain strength for keeping up ideals, strength for meeting crises, and strength for the daily routine.

The man who wrote our text looked up and saw the eagles flying through the air. "So would I rise," he said, "and soar in the higher atmosphere." We look up today and see men rising as on eagles' wings, and keeping up in the air with certain poise. What is the secret? Power. The famous flight of the Question Mark was possible only by finding out a way to renew its reserves of power. Let the engine stop, and down comes the plane, fortunate if it can land without a crash that means it can never mount again.

What a parable of our living. We are not balloons. We are "heavier-than-air machines." It takes *strength,* strength continually renewed, to keep our souls up in the higher atmosphere, true to honor, true to ideals, loyal to the best we know, faithful to our principles, never coming down to stay on the lower levels.

Tell me, you busy men and women,—no, confess it to your own consciences,—do you find it easy to keep yourself true to the highest, unwavering in devotion to your ideals?

You lawyers, is there nothing in what Mr. Hughes said so forcibly a few days ago? Is it easy in your profession to keep up in the higher atmosphere, above all quibblings and compromisings, up where, as Hooker so finely said, "law has its home in the bosom of God?" You physicians, do the ethics of your profession maintain themselves without care? Is it easy to be the eager, high-minded, unselfish servants of needy humanity you know you ought to be? You business men, is it always easy to let profit go when it can be gained by a slight paring or shading of honor? Can you without effort maintain a high and extreme integrity, and a real and deep interest in culture and beauty and friendship, amid the absorbing demands of business? You women, is it an easy task to be always gracious, kind, and just, to children and servants, amid the busy details of the home? Is it a simple matter to maintain real simplicity in the social life of our day, to be humble in the possession of wealth, and contented without it?

I know what your answer will be, if you have any wisdom at all. Unless you are hopelessly shallow and low-minded, you know what a struggle it takes to keep one's self true to the highest.

Then you cannot afford to neglect the practice of religion. Think what it means, to spend a morning hour or an afternoon hour once a week, where, through music, and the reading and exposition of the Bible, and prayer, and the quiet detachment of the service, you are brought into renewed consciousness of the beauty and glory of high ideals. To come to the sacrament and be reminded of Jesus, to come to the church and be reminded of God, is to have renewed in you strength to keep your soul up in the higher reaches of life, where you know you ought to be at home.

You remember the shopkeeper at Brighton, who kept in a little room back of his store a picture of Frederick W. Robertson? "When I am tempted," he said, "to do something mean, to take advantage of a customer, or to be unkind, I step back and look at that face." Friends, we come to church to look on a face more glorious and inspiring than that of any man. What may it not mean in your brave effort to maintain a high and fine idealism to come and meet God from time to time?

"They shall run, and not be weary." Life has its times when we must be like contestants in a race. Suddenly we face some tremendous demand.

Death takes the one you love best. Injustice or misunderstanding swoops down upon you, and you must somehow find grace to bear it without breaking. At such a moment we feel as if God Himself must wait and watch to see what we will do. Can you meet the emergency, stand the sudden strain, win the fierce fight?

What would it be worth to you to find a way of accumulating moral reserves, of getting strength in the soul sufficient to assure your victory in such critical moments? Well, that is what the practice of religion will do for you. I dare assert that faithful use of the means of religious devotion will build up your reserve power to meet moral and spiritual crises as surely as the best-approved course of hygiene and diet will build up physical resistance and reserve.

It is possible, of course, for one to stand up in his own strength and defy fate, if one is a hero. Henley has immortalized the one who is "master of his fate, captain of his soul," and can keep his head unbowed "beneath the bludgeonings of fate." But how many heroes do you know? How many are there who can thus maintain a brave front on a sudden and unassisted? A few days ago there came into my hands a sermon by a minister who preaches a religion without God, and calls himself a Humanist rather than a Christian. It is a sermon on "Meeting Trouble without God." With a sincerity one cannot help respecting, he pleads that we throw over the illusion that there is any God to help us, and just go out to meet trouble in the power of our own manhood. Henley's poem is his text, so far as he has one.

He gives a single illustration from modern life of what it means to meet trouble without God,—the way in which the late President William R. Harper, of Chicago University, in his forty-ninth year, faced a cruel death with unwavering courage and calmness.

As I read, I recalled vividly the day when William R. Harper came in where a little group of us were meeting and told us in a low voice that he had an incurable disease and must soon leave us. I know what sustained that man and gave him the victory. For years it has been to me one of the proofs of the power and glory of our religion. He asked one or two men whose Christian faith seemed most real and clear to come and talk with him; and with them he faced the whole problem of life and death; he made his plans for the future life as calmly and sensibly as he would have planned a trip to Europe; he sought God and found Him, and died as he had lived in the strength of friendship with the Unseen Father. "Meeting trouble without God?" To offer Wm. R. Harper as an example of that is like holding up Abraham Lincoln as an example of how to achieve success without character.

I have had an experience of nearly forty years in the ministry. In the course of it I have had the privilege of coming near to hundreds of people who were "in the fell clutch of circumstance," forced to deal with sorrow, loss, hardship, tragedy, at close range and on the instant. If anyone should ask me to say what has impressed me most vividly out of that experience, I would say,—the difference between those who have met trouble without God and those who have met trouble with God. Account for religion as you will, say what you please about it; this fact stands: that there is something in religion that holds in times of stress. You put your foot down and it touches solid rock. You fall back fainting and underneath are the everlasting arms. My friend, there are times coming in your life when it will be worth all it costs you to maintain the practice of religion, yes and a thousand times more, for the privilege then of drawing on God for what you need.

"They shall walk and not faint." Not alone in mystical flights and the higher life of ideals; not alone in crises and times that try men's souls; does the strength avail that

comes from the practice of religion. Of priceless value also is what religion does for us in keeping us well-poised, cheerful, strong, and true in the daily routine. It is simple fact, that we walk better through the whole week if we go to Church on Sunday, and keep up our practice of daily devotions. We do our work better, live our lives better, are happier and more helpful, for the practice of religion.

A man once came and said to me, "I want to join the church. I haven't any particular theology. I don't know what I believe. But I have found, by actual test, that when I go to church and pray I can do things I couldn't do otherwise, and I can keep from doing some things I would be likely to do otherwise." I am confident that any-one who would make a real and serious test would confirm that judgment.

Has religion a practical value? If it can do what this text says it can, what these lives say it can, is it not one of the essentials, the things you must have, whatever else you let go?

I know what some would answer: "You must prove to me that the practice of religion will do this." But there is just the trouble. I can't prove it to you. It is one of those vital matters that every man must test for himself. I can only say what the first disciples said when men asked what there was really in this Jesus and His way: "Come and see." Look around! Watch men and women! See whether those you respect the most for their steadfast idealism, their reserve strength, their quiet daily conduct and character, are not on the whole people who care about the things of God. And, most of all, try it yourself. If there is any likelihood that here in religion is personal power to live life well, it is worth your giving it a test.

One final word: you must give it a good long test.

God is not found in a moment. Religion is not like a drug, that exerts an instantaneous, but temporary effect. Religion is a steady pursuit. Health of soul is built up as health of body is built up. One trouble is that too often we go to God as, too often, we go to the physician, as a last resort, when all he can do is shake his head, and ask, "Why didn't you come sooner?" Browning tells of a man who, in a desperate peril, "caught at God's skirts, and prayed." Better that than nothing. But religion, real religion, is far more than catching at God's skirts in a crisis. How does the text describe those who shall renew their strength? "They that *wait upon* the Lord."

Religion has its best value for those who through years of steady practice store up in their souls grace to help in time of need. It may be that two young men, or two young women, came down the Avenue this morning. At the door of the church they halted. One came in to worship, the other went on to take a walk, to call on a friend, to do any one of a number of things. Now you may ask me, "If you should inspect each of those two tomorrow, could you tell which of them had been to church today?" No; probably not. But let them keep on doing that, week after week, year after year, one keeping up the practice of religion and the other neglecting it, and anyone could tell the difference.

At one of the stormy sessions of our General Assembly, Dr. George Alexander spoke in his gracious, kindly, firm fashion. The Assembly voted him down. Later a little group of young men came up to me, and introduced themselves as representatives of the press. One of them exclaimed, with utmost enthusiasm, "Say, isn't that Dr. Alexander fine? I wish you'd tell him, that, if he wants anything from us, he can have it." It was impossible to let the opportunity slip, and I said, "Boys, do you know what has made him such a man? It's because he has prayed all his life long."

It is when you thus watch those who patiently and eagerly for many years have kept up the practice of religion, that you appreciate its value and beauty. How was it that William R. Harper could face cruel pain and swift death coming upon him at the very height of his powers and usefulness? Was it just that he "caught at God's skirts" in his agony? No! It was because for many years he had lived and walked with God, so that it was the simplest thing in the world to turn to God in the hour of his great need. Jesus met the cross and out of it won the salvation of man and the glory of God, not through the sudden resolution of a heroic soul, but as the perfect climax of a life that from the beginning to the end never for a moment lost sight of God.

There are many rich and glorious helps to a high and honorable and blessed life. But of them all there is none more practically valuable than the strength that comes from the habit of walking with God and waiting upon God, which equips one to say:—"I have set the Lord always before me; because He is at my right hand, I shall not be moved. Yea, though I walk through the valley of the dark shadow, I will fear no evil, for Thou art with me."

STEWARDSHIP—A MESSAGE FOR OUR DAY

ALBERT W. BEAVEN

The recent election of Albert W. Beaven to the presidency of the Northern Baptist Convention comes in recognition of a ministry which has been marked by administrative competence. During his distinguished pastorate at the Lake Avenue Baptist Church, Rochester, he developed a plan of comprehensive church activity which attracted wide attention and later became the substance of his book, *Putting the Church on a Full Time Basis*. He has lectured on church management at Union Seminary in New York, and at the summer school of the Evangelical Synod, Dunkirk. He is now president of the Colgate-Rochester Theological Seminary. He has appeared as university preacher at Cornell, Yale, University of Chicago, Wellesley and other notable schools.

Dr. Beaven was born in Idaho in 1881, the son of a Baptist minister. He received his A.B. degree from Shurtleff College in 1906 and was graduated from Rochester Theological Seminary in 1909. Both Shurtleff and Rochester later conferred upon him the degree of doctor of divinity. He contributes frequently to church periodicals and besides the book mentioned above is the author of *The Fine Art of Living Together*.

STEWARDSHIP—A MESSAGE FOR OUR DAY

"For the kingdom of heaven is as a man travelling in a far country who called his own servants and delivered unto them his goods . . .; to every man according to his ability . . .; and straightway took his journey. . . . After a long time the Lord of those servants cometh and reckoneth with them . . . he that had received five talents came and brought other five talents. . . . His Lord said unto him, Well done thou good and faithful servant: thou hast been faithful over a few things, I will make thee ruler over many things: enter thou into the joy of thy Lord. . . . Then he which had received the one talent came and said, Lord, I knew thee that thou art an hard man, and I was afraid and went and hid thy talent in the earth. . . . His Lord answered. . . . Take therefore the talent from him and give it unto him which hath ten talents and cast ye the unprofitable servant into outer darkness."

Matthew 25-14-30

The message which Jesus brought is many sided. As succeeding ages have shown differing needs, the parts of that message that met those needs, have been stressed. In times of disaster and plague its note of comfort has been proclaimed, in times of peril and persecution, its inspiration to courage and endurance, and in times of hardship and poverty its message of fullness of the inner life and the hope of the hereafter has come to the fore. The need of the special time has tended to call forth the peculiar resources of his teachings that answered to those needs.

By that same token this is a day when we should face Jesus' great doctrines as they bear on the use of power. Power in various forms is all about us. We live in a land which has become a world power, it exerts great political and financial influence. Our personal experiences are gained amid scenes of power. We are familiar with powerful machines, tremendous engines, mammoth steamers, gigantic airships. Our combinations of capital are staggering in size. Our wealth is almost fabulous when compared with the scale on which the people of other nations live. Our children are familiar from childhood with power that while a commonplace to them would seem shocking to our forbears and does seem so to the rest of the world. It is with power, however, in its most concentrated and ubiquitous form that we have to deal most continually, and that form is money. The handling of our money becomes in a real sense, the school in which we are learning or not learning the attitudes we should take toward all other forms of power.

Nothing is more obvious also than that we have created all this power faster than we have created methods and ideals for its control. If therefore Christianity has a message that can guide an age when power is being flung at us in ever new forms, now is the time for such phase of the gospel to be proclaimed.

There is such a body of teachings in Jesus' great doctrine of stewardship. There He lays down principles and conceptions that are profoundly helpful and necessary to supplement our ever increasing power and make it a blessing and not a curse. By a peculiar good fortune also it concentrates particularly in the place where our problem is most acute, namely power in the form of money.

Jesus dealt with this subject far more than most people dream. It has been pointed out that one out of every six verses in the gospels of Matthew, Mark and Luke, bear on the subject of stewardship. In these treatments Jesus outlined a pretty clear program of action for one willing to follow it.

Possibly no one of his parables illustrates those great underlying assumptions better than the parable of the talents as we have outlined it in the scripture on which we comment. In essence that teaching is as follows; It is *His* money that we handle, not ours; we are stewards of it to achieve results for *Him;* our handling of it is a test of our attitude toward Him; by the way we handle it we fit ourselves for controlling the larger values of life here and hereafter; ultimately, we turn it all back and give an account of our handling of it to Him.

While this particular parable deals with money, as has been pointed out, it is applicable to all forms of power, influence, gifts of speech, leadership, writing, invention, organization and strength in its myriad forms.

Let us thank God that Jesus said so much and such definite things about money; this makes religion very practical. Money plays an insistently important place in all our lives. This is not necessarily because as some insinuate, we are "money mad," but we are constantly using it as a measuring stick of achievement. A raise in salary does not simply mean more money, it means a recognition by others of our accomplishments, a stamp of approval on our work. Day by day almost every transaction made or service rendered in the business world and in other spheres is measured in terms of money.

We want it for the things for which it stands and for what it can purchase. We work, and our work is transformed into money as pay, it figures in our pleasure and our pain, our plans and our hopes, our temptations and our inspirations. It can bless us or curse us and we can use it to dam others or lift them to the seventh heaven. It is power concentrated and any religion that had nothing to say about money, no guidance as to the attitude we should take toward it would be sadly detached from life. Let us follow the assumptions of this parable as it illustrates Jesus' teachings.

The Kingdom of Heaven is as a man travelling into a far country who called unto him his servants, and delivereth unto them *his* goods. The master starts where the Old Testament starts, "In the beginning God." *"His* goods"—God's ownership——this is the note sounded again and again. "God made the world and all things therein." "The silver is mine and gold is mine," saith Jehovah of Hosts. "The world is mine and the fullness thereof." "Remember Jehovah thy God for it is He that giveth thee power to get wealth." "Beware lest ye forget Jehovah thy God—Lest when thou hast eaten and art full and thou hast built thyself goodly houses—then thy heart be lifted up and thou forget Jehovah thy God." Thus the older writers laid broad foundations and Jesus built upon them. What a cartoon he drew to show the folly of the man who assumed otherwise when he painted the picture of the rich fool.

God the owner, this is where we need to start. It is hard for us to do it. We are so certain of our own ownership. *My money, my property!* these are the expressions of our modern possessive attitude. "This great Babylon that I have built" is an ancient expression we can appreciate more easily than some other passages we have quoted.

But as usual Jesus was right. Are we the real owners? Consider it from any standpoint. Any one who thinks must see the fallacy of our assumptions of sheer ownership. How many who before a certain crash in the stock market were so certain they owned wealth now find themselves penniless. If they owned, where is the solidity of that ownership?

But another fact will shatter confidence in our ownership. The power to tax is the power to destroy. If a government can tax us, and most of us are conscious that it can when we see income taxes, property taxes, inheritance taxes, and other ways of taxation, increasing, how sure are we that we own in completeness? Many persons in Russia assumed before the war that they owned their property; they have no such illusion now.

Again the last war is not so far back that we have forgotten some things. Our children and our lives are worth more than money, let need arise and the government may pass a draft law, and what is ours today may be the government's tomorrow. And if we go to war again, and the government should extend the draft principle, as I think it should, so that it controls not only the lives of those who go to the front, but the property of those who remain at home, then truly we would see how easily this certainty of our ownership would prove a mirage.

But we can approach this from another angle. Let us get a longer perspective. Our ownership at best is simply having our hands on money for a short time. "We had nothing when we came into this world." We will take nothing when we leave. In our little walk across the stage of life, between the entrance we call birth and the exit we call death, we may fill our arms till they strain to hold all we have accumulated but when we come to the other side, the doorway called death never opens widely enough to enable us to take a cent with us as we pass through. "How much did he leave?" asked one person of another about a wealthy friend who had died. "He left it all," was the reply. So do we all.

Shrewd as are our plans about controlling it by law after we go, life is full of illustrations of the futility of even that idea of ownership. Wills broken, bequests misused, lawyers' purses fattened, money left to children squandered and dissipated. Nothing seems so clear as the danger which attaches to passing easy money to children who have not been carefully trained to use it or who have not been disciplined by the experiences incidental to earning it.

Ours, we say. It wasn't one hundred years ago! It won't be one hundred years from now! Life itself teaches us that Jesus' fundamental assumption is right. At least we aren't the owners. At best we have control of it but for a time. We are like the group of old—"He has called us unto Him and delivered unto us *His* goods."

But the second principle which the master brings out in the parable is just as clear. If man does not own, at least he is a steward. The goods are delivered to him, he can increase or ignore them, he can use or misuse them. He has the right to say what will be done while he has them under his power.

This is the thrilling side of it all. Every man stands at the threshold of his life experience with certain assets given to him to handle as a steward. His body, mind, personality, ability to lead, to organize, to plan, dream, and accomplish, these combine to give him "the power to get wealth"—all these are to be his—*for a time*. He can use them solely for self, he can crush and exploit others, push them down to help him up, and leave a trail of suffering behind him. Many have followed this method. He can follow it if he will, but let him never forget that there is another chapter, "The Lord of those servants cometh." What a man does for these short days or years while he does have his hands on the assets, determines *him* as well as the *assets*.

Evidently from the teaching of Jesus a man's handling of things is a school in which he is being tested as to his ability to handle larger things. "Well done good and faithful servant. Thou hast been faithful in a few things, I will make thee ruler over many things," was the way the story read about the good steward. "Take therefore the talent from him, cast ye the unprofitable servant into outer darkness" was the end of the story of the man whose only use of the assets delivered to him was dictated by his own indolent pleasure and a self righteous indifference to the opportunities that go with stewardship.

A man's use of his money can make or break him as well as the money. He can expand in all his capacities or he can shrivel up to the despicable condition which was portrayed in the other story where the rich farmer, gloating over things, offering to feed his immortal soul with corn, indifferent to every true value, was held up to piercing scorn by the Son of Man when he said, "Thou fool, this night shall thy soul be required of thee and then whose shall these things be."

The eternal possibilities of good in its proper use are hinted at in the parable of the unjust steward and especially in the closing admonition, "Therefore make to yourselves friends of the mammon of unrighteousness that when ye fail they may receive you into everlasting habitations." We have deeply embedded in the words of Jesus, this teaching that the results upon us of the use of our money extend much farther than would first appear, indeed reach far down our trail as we go on in the eternal journey of the soul.

Man is a steward of his money. This is the essential fact which Jesus discloses, and it is for us to follow through the implications of that central principle.

One of the first things we can see in the light of the main principle is that the attitude of stewardship will extend to all parts of a man's relation to his money, his power to get it as well as control it and dispose of it. No amount of good giving will atone for continued indifference to the way we get our money. It is God that giveth us the *power to get* wealth.

It would naturally follow also that in our *handling* of our money our attitude is governed by the same sense of relationship to God. We use it for His great purposes, its use gets its value in the light of those purposes. Therefore it is not our pleasure but His cause that comes *first*. There can be little doubt that it was to impress this basic attitude that the Old Testament stressed the offering of the first fruits. Without much question also, it is here we come into sight of the value of tithing. We lose its meaning when we try to see it as a legal requirement; we find its place when we note the practical usefulness of the custom of first setting aside a tenth for God. As the full discharge of legal obligation it is absurd and leads to hypocrisy, as the regular acknowledgment of and developer of an inner attitude of stewardship, it is a most valuable thing. To say we are stewards and have no time nor place nor regularity of showing this is as absurd as to rent a house and have no time nor place nor method of paying the rent or to give a mortgage and then pay the interest if our mood or convenience happen to dictate.

Common sense would require, that if our sense of stewardship of possession is real we work out some sensible way of outwardly indicating our inner attitude and of seeing that the possessions that pass into our hands are used for the advancement of His purposes. Dedicating first one tenth for these purposes, is at least a practical method, a way of beginning and as such we can advocate it wholeheartedly.

What we set aside should certainly be in proportion to what we get, if we get more it should be more and a tenth is little enough as a starter for most any man who is serious in his convictions about God's ownership. A tenth is not too big for our Christian Science friends, it is not too much for Mohammedans to advocate, it certainly was embedded in Jewish teaching, it is certainly a pretty small procedure for us as Christians to acknowledge blandly the superior blessings of the religion of Jesus Christ and then proceed to beat down the proportion we set aside below that widely accepted as a minimum by people of other faiths which we do not admit have the values nor validity nor fullness which ours has.

The only peril of a tenth is in accepting it as a substitute for, not an acknowledgment of, the inner life attitude of stewardship. If it is the latter then it is taken as it should be as a proportion to be increased as fast as possible, and as an indication of the feeling of responsibility that we have about not only that amount but all of which we are in control at present.

There is however a positively thrilling side of the attitude of stewardship; it lifts one into partnership with the Creator of the universe in the accomplishment of his eternal purpose. Instead of being, like children on the beach, makers of sand houses, to be washed away by the next wave, we become part builders of eternal structures, like the sculptors of the middle ages who put their souls into the figures they carved, for these were to be a part of a cathedral that would stand for centuries. Through his use of his possessions a steward steps among the immortals.

Still another phase of stewardship brings exhilaration, the unlimited possibility of the portion dedicated because of God's addition to that which we use for the work of His Kingdom. Through our giving we become partners with God. Man may make something that looks like an acorn, but it takes the mystic touch of God upon matter to give it the life by which it utilizes the resources of nature, the sun, the rain, and soil and so becomes the giant oak. By partnership with nature the acorn becomes the tree; alone it begins to decay. The selfish man is like the Hebrew children who hoarded the manna. What he clung to became not a resource but an offense, the steward is like the grain of wheat of which Jesus spoke, "if it fall unto the ground and die it bringeth forth much fruit."

As a practical matter also it is here that we find an explanation why "giving" as we call it becomes an inspiration and not an irritation to the steward. There is always a mysterious plus added to what he sets aside. Nor is this addition which comes through the unseen partner, something that even the most matter of fact person can fail to see.

Where else can a man invest his money, if we can think for a moment of our giving as an investment, and get so much added to it. In order to strengthen the forces which make his community a better place in which to live he puts his money into the local work of the average church and usually he gets some such results as these. He has the privilege of seeing at work for the community-ends not only the money he puts in, but his giving inspires others to give; more than that, he finds these gifts are further increased for present service by buildings and equipment contributed by devoted people gone before him, many long since dead but their gifts stand along with his to fight the present day fight for right.

Again usually because it is a church and the man they pay to minister there is a servant of the Master, their gifts will buy a great deal more leadership than the same amount of money would in other fields of effort. Still further, when that minister puts in his time, he can inspire more volunteer work in proportion to the paid staff in his church than he could if he were in almost any other institution known; and best of all after the minister and others whom his money has helped to secure and the volunteer workers they call in have done their part, often the divine partner takes their work and doubles and quadruples it by the mystic ministrations of His spirit.

Or take the money a man puts into the world missionary projects included in the average church budget. Where else can he buy for the same money an interest in a more widely diversified list of redemptive projects. By that money he steps alongside the worker in the slums of a great city, the teacher in the mountains of Kentucky, the missionary statesman moulding empires in the changing Orient. In a real sense through his money he is giving himself for a time as an aid in places he can never go in body. He is doing things he can never do in person, and blessing lives he will never see till that marvelous meeting of the friends in "the eternal habitations" of which Jesus long ago spoke. But again in every place where that man's money goes, it will be working not through a novice such as he would be but usually through a trained worker who has put in years getting ready for efficient service and who will serve at pay that would hardly equal an expense account for the original giver. This representative will work not sporadically as the donor would probably have to, but will stay there year in and year out to follow up the work and make it permanent. He will not work alone with the uncertainty and perils of isolation but will be related to some strong ongoing organization which can train and inspire those who serve; and best of all the giver will find as a result of it all some of the most remarkable achievements of God's grace in the souls of men, that will transcend all that any man had a right to expect as the result of mere money put into it.

We do not contend that every project so carried is a

marvelous success but any fair comparison of what the average Christian steward gets for his money through the work done by the noble and self-sacrificing missionaries of the church of Jesus Christ, as contrasted with what he gets for his money anywhere else, will make clear what we mean when we say, The man who takes the attitude of stewardship and uses his possessions accordingly is due for a thrilling experience as he comes to realize the glorious partnership possibilities of his relationship.

Would God more of us as Christians were stewards impelled by motives from within rather than irritated supporters nagged by pressure from without!

The third teaching of Jesus we emphasize as we close, is the accountability of the steward. "The Lord of those servants cometh" each one comes to make his report, each one is judged in the light of what he had given to him and by the use he made of it.

This parable is followed by the story about the judgment, closing with the saying of the judge, "In as much as ye did it not unto one of the least of these my brethren, ye did it not unto me." These two form a picture too clear for us to ignore. Whatever allowance we may make for oriental imagery or figurative language, there is no dodging the plain implications of Jesus' words.

Evidently, in some future time, in a sense that is real, we are called to give an account to God. This brings each act, even now, under supervision. It adds a new meaning to every humble or important act. The cup of cold water given to "one of the least of these" becomes not simply a gift to the Master, but an item to be reviewed in the great experience to which the parable refers.

The import of this for daily living, is that it tends to turn that future light on today's use of our talents; it all stands out now in the presence of God. Probably nothing could help us to see the worthiness or unworthiness of a certain decision in regard to possessions, more completely, than to bring it and all the motives which surround it out into the light of God's presence. Things look so differently there. An act that seems simply prudent to us seems inordinately selfish in that light. A transaction that we ordinarily pride ourselves upon as shrewd appears questionable and must be abandoned when that light falls on it.

It would be a great thing for our American life if our almost complete acceptance of the profit motive as the only drive for industry could be dragged out into the open, and the white light of this point of view be turned on it. Dividends and unemployment, vast wealth and abject poverty standing side by side, might not leave us as complacent as now.

On the other hand the thrill of service, the use of power for others' blessing, the dedication of wealth for the Master's tasks, the glory of partnership with God in great enterprises of the Kingdom, all these seem to stand out as immensely wise and far-sighted.

God is the owner—we are stewards. May we so grasp these principles and live by them, that when we come to the final review of life, again the olden words will be appropriate, "Well done good and faithful servant, enter thou into the joy of thy Lord."

THE RECOVERY OF PENTECOST

Ralph W. Sockman

"But ye shall receive power when the Holy Spirit is come upon you."

Acts i.8

Like so many other prominent men in the American pulpit today, Ralph W. Sockman was graduated from Ohio Weslyan. He was born at Mount Vernon, Ohio, in 1889, received his bachelor's degree from Ohio Weslyan in 1911, his master's from Columbia in 1913 and his Ph.D. from Columbia University in 1917. In 1916 he was graduated from Union Theological Seminary and since 1917 he has been minister of the Madison Avenue Methodist Church, New York. His church is perhaps the strongest of his denomination in the metropolitan area. Dr. Sockman has won national attention through his radio addresses.

His latest book, published this fall, is *The Morals of Tomorrow*. He is the author also of *Suburbs of Christianity and Other Sermons* and *Men of the Mysteries*.

THE RECOVERY OF PENTECOST

"But ye shall receive power when the Holy Spirit is come upon you."

Acts i.8

In the ecclesiastical calendar Pentecost is the birthday of the Christian Church. In the birth of a child there is life within the little body before it emerges into the external world, but only after the moment of its appearance does it exist as a separate entity. Similarly the Church of Christ existed in embryo before the day of Pentecost, but the life which animated the Twelve came from physical contact with Jesus. It was not until that significant hour fifty days after the crucial Passover that the company of Christ took visible form and breath of its own. If Michelangelo had chosen to depict the "Creation of the Church" as he did the "Creation of Adam," he would have painted the Pentecostal scene in Jerusalem. It was then and there that the prediction was fulfilled: "Ye shall receive power when the Holy Spirit is come upon you."

Yet despite the significance of the event, Pentecost is not a popular anniversary in the churches of the western world. It does not approach in public favor the rank of Easter or Christmas. Not even the recent concerted effort to celebrate its nineteen hundredth anniversary stirred the church widely or deeply. This attitude toward Pentecost serves as a spiritual barometer of our ecclesiastical weather. It behooves us therefore to ask why the church registers so low an appreciation of so vital an event, and to consider how it can recover the secret of that radiant hour which gave it birth.

135

One reason that Pentecost has no stronger appeal is that it is the birthday of an institution which is itself none too popular. The Church of Christ has far less hold on the hearts of men than has the Person of Christ. Few indeed are those who fail to show some admiration and reverence for Jesus of Nazareth, but many are the critics, even the foes, of the Church. In the halls of more than one labor union is to be found the likeness of the Nazarene Carpenter, but organized labor is recognized as generally hostile to the church. Multitudes share the feeling of a contemporary novelist who accuses the ecclesiastical institution of fettering the free and spontaneous spirit of its Founder. Some there are who see the church as a socially futile organization shifting the focus of its members from the real problems of this world to the contemplation of a future felicity in another. Some, on the other hand, see it as too much immersed in earthly affairs, meddling in political and industrial issues far beyond its legitimate field.

Even within the church is a visible lack of devotion to it. Hosts of Protestant members treat the church as if it belonged to them rather than as if they belonged to it. To such it seems an obligation assumed, a burden to be supported, not a privilege to be appreciated. Hence the celebration of the church's natal day arouses about as much enthusiasm in the minds of these members as the anniversary of the passage of the income tax law.

In some quarters, however, there are signs of an awakening interest in the church as an institution. A keen young Danish diagnostician of spiritual conditions recently reported that the European scene reveals some circles of youth turning toward the church as a possible object of devotion. The young people of the war-swept areas are coming to realise that the mere release from old fetters which was effected twelve years ago does not constitute real freedom. Freed spirits must find new loyalties in order to have fulness of life. Consequently some are attaching themselves to the service of their economic class, as in Russia. Others are manifesting an amazing devotion to the state in a revival of nationalism as in Germany and Italy. Still others are looking wistfully at the church wondering if it may not offer a worthy objective for their enlistment.

American youth, we believe, is due to make a similar discovery. The glaring defects of institutional religion can not continue to blind men to the necessity of ecclesiastical organization. In a day when every human activity must be organized in order to be effective, it is utterly futile to think that religion can be made socially dynamic or morally progressive without organization. But the logic of its necessity must be supplemented with a gratitude for its service. If the church is to kindle a love in the hearts of men, it must be visioned as the faithful company which served as the custodian of Christ's precious words, preserving them in the gospels and translating them with painful toil in many a monastic cell and on many a missionary frontier. The church must be thought of not merely as the conventional worshippers who occupy their cushioned pews on a Sabbath morning but as the athletic spirits who have belted the globe in a divine relay, carrying the evangel across every ocean and to every nation. Devout souls emerging from the Catacombs to risk their lives in telling the Romans of their religion; Francis of Assisi espousing poverty in order to portray his Christ; Savonarola going to the gallows rather than give up his convictions; John Wesley consenting to be ostracized that he might preach to the miners under the open sky; circuit riding preachers shuttling in and out of the American frontier settlements weaving the silken strands of culture into the coarse texture of that rough world; great companies of glad-eyed children learning the old gospel stories and singing the soul-lifting hymns; hosts of aged bodies coming to the sanctuaries in order to glimpse a bit better their "house not made with hands, eternal in the heavens" —these and their like constitute the church of Christ.

To see the church in its true nature requires an historical imagination which can sweep the centuries. Such a view lifts the observer above the pettiness of many a visible churchman and the provincialism of many a local parish. Seen in that light the church appears as the body of Christ dearer to him than the body slain on Calvary because designed to carry on his message and work when his earthly lips were silenced. To all who can catch that glimpse, Pentecost, the birthday of the church, will become an anniversary of high significance.

A second necessity in recapturing the appeal of Pentecost is a better comprehension of the event itself. Very often our thinking steers clear of that Jerusalem scene because the proceedings seem so hard to understand. The author of Acts thus describes the day of Pentecost: "Suddenly there came from heaven a sound as of the rushing of a mighty wind, and it filled all the house where they were sitting. And there appeared unto them tongues, parting asunder, like as of fire; and it sat upon each one of them. And they were all filled with the Holy Spirit, and began to speak with other tongues, as the Spirit gave them utterance." Such phenomena sound so unreal to our modern ears.

There is mystery about the event and there will probably always continue to be, inasmuch as the idioms of language make it impossible for the western mind to know precisely what the oriental tongue was trying to tell. We can, however, unravel the fringes of the mystery by some of our modern experiences. We have seen men so filled with divine fervor that their faces become aglow with a perceptible radiance. May that not give us some inkling of the New Testament meaning of the fire which "sat upon each one of them" at Pentecost? We have heard, too, the catching of the breath when emotion sweeps an audience. Listen to the newspaper account of a Paderewski matinée. "There is a rustling of programs, a waving of fans, a nodding of feathers, a general air of expectancy, and the lights are lowered, a hush. All eyes are turned to a small door leading on to the stage; it is opened, Paderewski enters. A storm of applause greets him, . . . but after it comes a tremulous hush, and a prolonged sigh . . . created by the long deep inhalation of upward of three thousand women." May it not be that this suggests something of what the writer of Acts meant by the "sound as of the rushing of a mighty wind"?

We do not presume, of course, to say that such meager parallels approach in fulness of meaning the Pentecostal language. But they should suffice to suggest that the "wind" and "fire" may be understood in other than a physical, external sense. Pentecost must be interpreted spiritually for it marked the descent of the Holy Spirit. It need not be avoided, therefore, because its scriptural portrayal is couched in material concepts which look like magic in the modern light. That epochal Jerusalem event is to be approached in our day with language similar to that used in "The Letters of Arthur George Heath" who fell in France during the war. With the premonition of death upon him, this fellow of New College, Oxford, wrote to his mother shortly before the end: "Life, in fact, is a quality rather than a quantity, and there are certain moments of real life whose value seems so great that to measure them by the clock, and find them to have lasted so many hours or minutes, must appear trivial or meaningless. Their power, indeed, is such that we can not properly tell how long they last, for they can color all the rest of our lives, and remain a source of strength and joy that you know can not be exhausted, even though you can not trace exactly how it works." Pentecost was one of those transcendent experiences which snatch life out of the hands of the clock. But while it outruns reason, it does not outrage reason. Pentecost was the power of human insight raised to a divine degree. As such modern minds can accept its historicity without fear of surrendering their intelligence.

And now if the appeal of Pentecost is to be recovered, a third phase of the situation remains to be faced. Not only must the necessity of the church be appreciated and the phenomena of its birth be better understood if we are to be thrilled by its natal day, but also the coming of the Holy Spirit must be made a practical factor in present day Christian living.

It is not so now. Doctors call into consultation other specialists but in general they would be inclined to smile at the suggestion of summoning spiritual assistance. Business men increasingly recognize the principle of human cooperation but there is not much evidence that they are counting more on their Silent Partner. Preachers are running their parishes with enlarged staffs and improved methods but many work as if there were no Holy Spirit. They trust only to finite things, wholly forgetful of the fact that

"Infinite power of God upholds us,
Infinite love of Christ enfolds us."

Our world is filled with benighted modern men who see only the scheme of charted law and ignore the grace of God, who are so enamored of the scientific method that they sneer at anything which outdistances reason, who close the windows of their minds to the light of faith which outshines logic. Such men are missing "the life which is life indeed."

We of the western world have stressed the active aspects of our Christianity. We have called men to great moral and social crusades. We have urged them to follow "the Jesus way of life." Ministers have sought to be captains of their parish companies, marshalling them into fighting formation against the forces of evil. But in flogging the weary wills of our churchmen we have overlooked too much the necessity of filling their spirits. The army of the Lord can not fight on an empty spirit. It shows unmistakable signs today of demoralisation due to lack of spiritual sustenance. It is imperative, therefore, that the church supplement its programs of parish activities with the intake of spiritual power. We must learn again the secret of that which the Christ promised to his disciples when he said "Ye shall receive power when the Holy Spirit is come upon you."

And the time would seem to be ripe for such a lesson. During the last quarter of a century we have been passing through what might be called the psychological era. In fairness we must acknowledge our debt to the psychologists. They have helped us to understand the processes of our minds. They have shown us how our minds respond to the stimuli which strike them. But they do not deal with the sources of those stimuli nor with the purposes and values of our responses. In short, they show us the instruments but not the incentives of mental activity. We are a generation grown introspective in analysing our desires and probing our instincts. There are signs that we are growing weary of this psychological self-analysis. There is a turning from Freud to Eddington and Jeans with their spacious outlooks on the external world. There seems to be a waning popularity of the psychological novel and the sex note in fiction. The vogue of the detective story may be superficial but it is a healthy sign that we are getting our eyes off our inner complexes to objective factors outside ourselves. In discovering that we must open the windows of our overheated minds to let in the influences larger than self that make for satisfaction, we may also rediscover "the power not ourselves that makes for righteousness."

Power has been made a veritable fetish by the modern man. We all seem to want it. But most of us try to generate it by running as the motor car charges its batteries. And to be sure, activity does beget enthusiasm and efficiency, but just as the batteries of a car can not go uncared for indefinitely, so the energies of a man's life can not go unreplenished forever. There must be times of waiting for the Spirit. There must be a cultivation of divine cooperation. Like the early trans-Atlantic steamers which also carried masts, we ought to hoist sail and catch the power from without as well as try to generate it from within. The people of Wales say of a preacher who possesses spiritual power that he has "hwyl" (pronounced "hoo-il"). The word suggests the boat becalmed in the bay whose sails become filled until it moves out from the shore where it can catch glimpses of the mountain peaks standing back from the coast. It is "hwyl" we sons of the psychological era need. It is "hwyl" the disciples at Pentecost had.

How they got it can not be clearly analysed. But for us to wait to make use of the Holy Spirit until we can explain fully its nature is as foolish as to refuse to hoist a sail until we can give a meteorological description of the wind or to refuse to turn on the light until we can define electricity. This much is clear, we can do what the disciples did in preparation for Pentecost. And what they were doing during those fifty days intervening between Calvary and Pentecost we can well imagine. They were probing their memories to recall the incidents of their comradeship with the Christ. They were communing with him ever and anon in their interludes of meditation. They were straining their minds to understand the mystery of his career and his reappearance. They were waiting in expectant mood for the coming of the heavenly visitant. And most of all they were bringing their wills into a state of surrender to that divine spirit when it should be revealed. Such was the apostolic preparation for Pentecost. Such must still be the method in the twentieth century.

There comes down to us from Scandinavian folklore the fable of a spider which slid down from a rafter in a barn to weave its web amid the shadows below the roof. One day as the spider was moving about the beautifully symmetrical lacework of its completed web, it came across the filament down which it had originally come. "What is this for?" asked the spider, and snapped it. Thereupon the web collapsed. The point of this parable for the church need not be elaborated. The ecclesiastical system may be woven with human skill most comprehensively and symmetrically, but if the divine connection down which it came be broken, the whole church creation will collapse. Not only must the appeal of Pentecost be recovered but the principles of it must be reapplied.

THE DEATH OF CHRIST

ROBERT G. LEE

"For Christ also hath once suffered for sins, the just for the unjust, that he might bring us to God, being put to death in the flesh."

1 Peter iii.18

Robert G. Lee, since 1928 pastor of the Bellevue Baptist Church, Memphis, Tennessee, is one of the outstanding leaders of the Southern Baptist Church. He has served successively the First Church, New Orleans, the Citadel Square Church, Charleston, and his present pastorate—all of them among the largest of his denomination. Among his brother ministers he is everywhere recognized as an exceptionally eloquent and forthright advocate of evangelical religion. In 1919 he received the degree of Ph.D. from the Chicago Law School. His undergraduate work was done at Furnam University, where he carried off honors in scholarship and oratory. He was ordained into the Baptist ministry in 1910.

He is the author of *Bothersome Families, From Feet to Fathoms, Lord, I Believe,* and of a book just published, *Beds of Pearls.*

THE DEATH OF CHRIST

"For Christ also hath once suffered for sins, the
just for the unjust, that he might bring us to
God, being put to death in the flesh."
                                    1 Peter iii.18

In the Bible, which comes to us drenched in the tears
of a million contritions, steeped in the prayers of many
saints, expounded by the greatest intellects and fragrant
with the faith of little children, stained with the blood
shed in the sands of the Colosseum, worn with the fingers
of agony and death, there are fewer sublimer statements
than this. In this text, a volume in a line, an ocean in a
cup, we see four great facts—the fact of sin, the fact of
a Saviour, the fact of a sacrifice, the fact of salvation.
"We have searched, so it is: hear it, and know thou it for
thy good" (Job 5:27).

I—*The fact of SIN.*

Sin is a state and refers to the depraved nature received
from Adam. Adam plunged into sin, and all the race of
mankind plunged with him—because Adam was the fed-
eral head of the race. Not only taint but guilt, not only
moral hurt but legal fault, man inherits from Adam. The
consequence of Adam's sin to the world is sin everywhere
—sin among all people for all time—till God gathers his
own into the city where no sin shall enter. "Wherefore as
by one man sin entered into the world, and death by sin;
and so death passed upon all men, for that all have
sinned" (Romans 5:12).

Sin has saddened human life and blackened human his-

147

tory from the garden of Eden to the present time. In Eden's garden sin burst upon the world at the foot of the tree of the knowledge of good and evil. A raging torrent, it swept through the world until every community from Adam until now has felt its pollution. You cannot change the geography of sin. Its habitat is everywhere. And always, "the wages of sin is death" (Romans 6:23).

The sin of man has been the grief of God from all eternity, for of Christ it is affirmed that he is "the Lamb slain from the foundation of the world" (Rev. 13:8). Paul, the apostle of God, the Aristotle and Demosthenes of the Jewish race, in one of the most awful and tragic utterances of the ages, declares that all the world is guilty before God (Romans 3:19). When King Saul said "I have sinned," when the prodigal, in remorse, said, "I have sinned," when Pharaoh said "I have sinned," when David said "I have sinned"—they all voiced the experience of all lands at the time of Christ. When the publican, refusing to lift up his face, and smiting on his breast, said, "God be merciful to me a sinner," he voiced the soul of all ages. Guilty before God.

"All men have sinned." That statement declares that men, *all* men everywhere, are guilty—consciously guilty, evilly guilty, terribly guilty, guilty with aggravations, guilty without excuse. *"All* we like sheep have gone astray; we have turned everyone to his own way" (Isa. 53:6)—not to God's way.

Sin, the causative element of all world suffering, is no idle fancy for picnic conversation, no innocent hallucination which circus clowns use to amuse fickle crowds, no mild case of measles for which street vendors of patent medicines claim a complete ten-day cure, no comedy which low comedians use to amuse the frivolous populace, no perfume which tickles our nostrils momentarily without hurt or shock, no light picture of an artist's dream. Sin, an opiate in the will, a frenzy in the imagination, a madness in the brain, a poison in the heart, is the darkest and most terrible fact in the universe of God! Sin, the intolerable burden of a soul that is destined to live forever, is a black darkness which invests man's whole moral being, and conceals from his vision everything that belongs to the highest and grandest realms of realities! Sin, a disease that has converted man into a lump of rottenness and a feast for "the worm that dieth not," is also a fiend that has bound man hand and foot, a fiend that is dragging him down sloping stairways to a region of eternal and infernal flames in the "dark prison house of outer darkness."

From such a power man can be delivered only by the personal intervention and act of a personal God of infinite mercy and might! The most fearful of all realities—SIN, God's enemy, man's destroyer!

That reality, the reality of sin and its deathly power, makes the gravest problem with which human thought has ever grappled.

Here is a disease that has laid its destroying hand upon every fibre of man's moral being. How can it be cured?

Here are immortal spirits bound with infernal fetters. How can these shackles be removed?

Here is loathsomeness worse than the rottenness of the grave. How can it be cleansed?

Here are beings in communion with fiends. How can they be transformed and lifted into fellowship with the angels?

Here is the great temple of humanity in ruins. Who can rebuild it and "make the glory of the latter house greater than the former"?

Here are two worlds—earth and heaven—separated by

a great gulf of darkness and horror. Who will span it with an available highway, so that angels may come to us and we may go to them?

From what quarter can help come to the sinner in his bondage, sorrow, and night? In his shameful failure and loss? The world's sin we confront. And it is the atoning for a whole world guilty before God that constitutes the problem.

And who is sufficient for this? Man? No. Those who seem to have been holiest, have ever been those who saw their inability to help themselves. Job was called a perfect man. But he says, "I abhor myself in the presence of the holy God." And John the Baptist, the seer who saw clearly, the hero who dared valiantly, the great heart who felt deeply, who feared nothing except to displease God, said that he needed to be baptized of Jesus (Matt. 3:14). And Peter, the mighty preacher of Pentecost, said, "I am a sinful man, O Lord!" In man is there help for us? Must our help come from God? Is there other refuge?

To all these questions, different forms of the great question which the apostles answered on the day of Pentecost, "What must I do to be saved?" there is but one answer—and we find that answer in Jesus Christ—the Saviour. This brings us to consider

II—*The fact of A SAVIOUR.*

This Saviour, *our* Saviour, is Jesus of Nazareth—literature's loftiest ideal, philosophy's highest personality, criticism's supremest problem, theology's fundamental doctrine, spiritual religion's cardinal necessity. Jesus, whose name blossoms on the pages of history like the flowers of a 1000 springtimes in one bouquet. Jesus, whose name sounds down the corridors of the centuries like the music of all choirs, visible and invisible, poured forth in one anthem. Jesus—Son of man. Jesus—Son of God. And both in one. Jesus, the Word—God heard; Jesus, the Light—God seen; Jesus, the Life—God felt. Jesus—the outstanding miracle of all the ages.

Irreproachable this Saviour in his life. His life on earth was a thrilling record of goodness—goodness shining through every feature, goodness suggesting every thought, goodness ennobling every action, goodness clothing every utterance. His life, beyond all doubt, was the biography of perfume, the abundant overflow of graciousness, the thrill of the uncatalogued, the utterance of the unlanguaged! His life ever possessed the white stainlessness of sinlessness. To his enemies he said, "Who convinceth me of sin?" (John 8:46).

Mighty was this Saviour as a miracle worker. Astonishing all his miracles. Blind men he gave sight, deaf men keen ears, dumb men new tongues, crippled men new limbs. Crazy men he restored to reason. Lepers he cleansed. Outcast women he lifted up. Devils he cast out. The sick he healed. Funeral processions he broke up!

Jesus—teacher astonishingly marvelous. "Never man spake like this man" (John 7:46). Put the teachings of all philosophers alongside the teaching of Jesus. The difference? Their teaching is speculation; his, revelation. Their's inqairy; his, declaration. Their's surmise; his, certainty. Their's groping; his, guidance. For boldness of conception, for grandeur of character, for sublimity of purpose, for originality of mind, for valiant propagandism, his teaching, no exhausted specific, claims the sovereignty of the world. Amid all teachers, Jesus shines like the blazing sun amid lanterns.

But all these—his life, his teaching, his example, his miracles—would have availed nothing for our salvation had they not been consummated in the Cross.

Not by these did he repair the insulted dignity of God's nature by a reparation equal in merits to the character of the insulted dignity itself.

All these were incidental and collateral to the one purpose for which he came into the world—the purpose to die, to die that man born once and born dead might be born again and born alive.

Only by suffering the death which was expiatory with reference to God, which was punishment with reference to man, did he adequately compensate God's government by an equivalent for man's offence, offer a boundless mercy in terms consistent with the integrity of the moral law. In death, he paid our debt. "The Lord hath laid on him the iniquity of us all" (Isa. 53:6).

Jesus is more than an ideal man. If he is simply an ideal man showing by his own manner of living how others ought to live, he is not the real Saviour that we need. If he does no more for us than to show us, by a life without spot or blemish, how to live, he does not compass our necessities. If he is only a teacher of divine truth—a finger board to do no more than *point out* the way of righteousness—he does not compass our necessities. If he is only a *teacher* of the way of salvation he himself is not salvation. Be he only a pedagogue, or schoolmaster, he does not touch or supply the deepest necessities of man's condition. Such can never save man from the power and consequences of sin.

And this brings us to consider

III—*The fact of SACRIFICE.*

"God commendeth his love toward us in that while we were yet sinners Christ died for us" (Romans 5:8).

"While we were enemies, we were reconciled to God by the death of his Son" (Romans 5:10).

Such a height human love never reached. "His own self bear our sins in his own body on the tree" (I Peter 2:24).

Foretold from Eden downwards, this sacrifice is the greatest sacrifice of all the ages. The bruising by the serpent of the promised seed foretold it. Of this sacrifice the coats of skin made by Jehovah for Adam and Eve spake. This sacrifice Abel's accepted offering prefigured. To the sacrifice of Christ the sacrifice of Isaac pointed. The Paschal lamb, the sprinkled blood on the door posts (Exodus 12:13), foreshadowed Christ—"Christ, our passover sacrificed for us" (I Cor. 5:7). The sacrifices for sins and trespasses, the burnt offerings and the peace offerings, were finger posts to Calvary. The brazen serpent, as Jesus pointed out, symbolized the Son of man lifted up on the Cross. The sacrifices of the Old Testament had no value as "shadows of the true," enabling God to "pass over" the sins of the faithful, until the substitutional sacrifice should be offered up.

> "Not all the blood of beasts
> On Jewish altars slain,
> Could give the guilty conscience peace,
> Or wash away the stain.
>
> But Christ, the heavenly Lamb,
> Takes all our sins away,
> A sacrifice of nobler name,
> And richer blood than they!"

Thus we see that the Cross was substitutionary. On the Cross, where the history of human guilt culminates, he was wounded for our transgressions. On the Cross, where the purposes of divine love are made intelligible, he was bruised for our iniquities. As our substitute on the Cross, where the majesty of the law is vindicated, he bore the penalty of our transgressions and iniquities. "Who his own self bare our sins in his own body on the tree" (I Peter 2:24). Only as a substitute could he have borne them. As Abraham offered the ram *instead* of Isaac his son, so "Christ was offered once to bear the sins of man" (Heb. 7:27).

"The Father sent the Son to be the Saviour of the world" (I John 4:14). And his work as Saviour was accomplished on the Cross when he said "It is finished!" He was Saviour by the sacrifice of himself.

The sinner can only meet mercy where the claims of justice have been met. And this is at Calvary. In the cross of Christ's atonement, where the majesty of the law is vindicated, every sin is met, every darkness dispelled, every sin killed. In Christ's cross, where the problem of human redemption is solved, every question is answered, every foe defeated, every fear quenched, every hope met, every longing fulfilled, every sorrow assuaged, every promise kept.

Christ hath merited righteousness for as many as are found in him. "Him who knew no sin he made to be sin in our behalf; that we might become the righteousness of God in him" (II Cor. 5:21). In other words, Jesus on the cross, where the serpent's head is bruised, made up before God for all we failed to do and to be. On Calvary, where our death sentence is revoked, God dealt with him as he must deal with sin—in severe and unrelenting judgment. At the cross, where our condemnation is lifted, Jesus, so finely strung, so unutterably keyed to truth, mercy, justice, and love, became for us all that God must judge that we through faith in him might become all that God cannot judge. And in *him* God findeth us, if we be *believers,* for by *believing* we are incorporated unto Christ.

For the only adequate substitute is Jesus—the Jesus who was prefigured by the ever-flowing streams of red sacrificial blood—the Jesus who was foreshadowed by millions of offerings on countless altars slain—the Jesus foretold by the prophets since the world began! The very same Jesus upon whom, in the fulness of time, John the Baptist looked, and saw how all the sacrifices, and all the altars, and all the prophecies met and ended, and to whom John the Baptist pointed and of whom he spoke, saying, "Behold the Lamb of God who taketh away the sin of the world!" (John 1:29).

What a wonderful Saviour!

> "No mortal can with him compare
> Among the sons of men;
> Fairer is he than all the fair
> Who fill the heavenly train.

> "He saw me plunged in deep distress,
> And flew to my relief;
> For me he bore the shameful cross,
> And carried all my grief!"

And this brings us now to consider--with no little joy

IV—*The fact of SALVATION.*

Salvation for the lost. The lost compose the boundless constituency of Jesus. Call him the Son of Abraham—and you speak truth. But he was more. Call him the Son of David—and the truth you speak. But he was more. Call him the Son of Mary—and you speak the truth. But he was more than that!

Someone said something like this: "Those who called him the Son of Abraham imposed upon him a *racial* limitation. Those who called him the Son of David imposed upon him a *kingly* limitation. Those who called him the Son of Mary imposed upon him a *domestic* limitation. He shook himself free from them all and cried, 'The Son of man is come to seek and to save the lost'!" (Matt. 18:11).

"That which was *lost!*" This the constituency of Jesus. And to it there are no bounds or limitations—no masses, no classes, no old, no young, no high, no low, no rich, no poor, no wise, no ignorant. But wherever in this head-dizzy, body-weary, soul-sick, sin-smitten world the lost are found there is Jesus seeking to save.

Salvation for all! As one has said, though I may add or take from his words, for the lost monarch, with glittering crown, with mighty scepter, with ermine robes—lost in his fatal pride and independence. For the lost ne'er-do-well, tramping aimlessly through festering alley or along boulevard or over country roads—lost in carelessness and despair. For the lost son in his midnight carousals and debauches. For the lost daughter, shuddering in her humiliation and shame. For the lost loiterer lounging on the street corners. For the lost prisoner behind prison bars. For the lost scholar, dazed amid the splendid problems of his theories and philosophies! For the lost Pharisee, who, faultily faultless, icily regular, is too far lost to know that he is lost. For the lost ordinary man—lost *you,* lost *me.* For *all.* "Whosoever will." The availability of this sacrifice is for all.

> "That night when in the Judean skies
> The mystic star dispensed its light,
> A blind man moved in his sleep—
> And dreamed that he had sight!

> "That night when shepherd heard the song
> Of hosts angelic choiring near,
> A deaf man stirred in slumber's spell—
> And dreamed that he could hear!

"That night when in the cattle stall
Slept child and mother cheek by jowl,
A cripple turned his twisted limbs—
And dreamed that he was whole!

"That night when o'er the newborn babe
The tender Mary rose to lean,
A loathsome leper smiled in sleep—
And dreamed that he was clean!

"That night when to the mother's breast
The little King was held secure,
A harlot slept a happy sleep—
And dreamed that she was pure!

"That night when in the manger lay
The Sanctified who came to save,
A man moved in the sleep of death—
And dreamed there was no grave!"

Salvation for those blind in sin, for those deaf in sin, for those crippled in sin, for those dumb in sin, for those loathsome with the leprosy of sin, for those impure with the harlotry of sin, for those dead in trespasses and sin! For *all*. "And the Spirit and the bride say, Come. And let him that heareth say, Come. And let him that is athirst, Come. And whosoever will, let him take the water of life freely" (Rev. 22:17).

But how can the sinner avail himself of this great salvation?

God has but *one* plan of salvation. This Noah's ark teaches; there was just one place where folks were safe when God drowned the world. This Rahab's house teaches; there was only one place where Rahab and her kindred were safe when Joshua's army took the city—in the house with the scarlet rope in the window. This the brass serpent teaches; only by looking thereon were those bitten by serpents saved from death by poison. This the Passover teaches; only in the house where the blood was on the door posts the first-born died not. This the cities of refuge teach; being the only places where the pursued were safe. Jesus said, "I am the way, the truth, and the life; no man cometh unto the Father but by me" (John 14:6). And "I am the door: by me if any man enter in, he shall be saved" (John 10:9).

Such truth some hymns express:

> "What can wash away my sins?
> Nothing but the blood of Jesus."

> "Other refuge have I none,
> Hangs my helpless soul on thee."

> "Could my tears forever flow,
> Could my zeal no languor know
> All for sin cannot atone,
> Thou must save and thou alone."

This way excludes all ways. There is salvation in none other—in nothing else. Art says, "Salvation is not in me." Education says, "Salvation is not in me." So music. So superior culture. So environment. So science. So character. So heredity. So all these say!

Not by character are we saved. And that is not without faith, but it is faith in man—in one's self. All agree that character has immense value, but if we give it the value of salvation without the atoning blood of Jesus Christ we make, as Dixon says, a counterfeit of character for passing it for more than it is worth.

Nor are we saved by merely joining a church. There is no salvation by ecclesiasticism. One could have his name on all the church rolls in the land, and not have salvation.

But the church is the place for saved persons. And if outside is the place for a saved person, Christ made a mistake when he organized the church.

None are saved by baptism. Nor by partaking of the Lord's Supper. Both of these ordinances are symbolical and memorial. They do not save or help save a soul. A thousand times could one be baptized, but unless his faith rests in Christ who "bore our sins in his own body on the tree," he could not be saved. Though one partakes ten thousand times of the Lord's Supper, unless he trusts in the substitutionary death and meritorious righteousness of Jesus Christ, he cannot be saved. The ordinances are not vehicles of grace.

Not by good works are people saved. One works *from* the Cross as a saved person but not *to* the Cross as an unsaved person. "Not by works done in righteousness which we did ourselves, but according to his mercy he saved us, through the washing of regeneration, and renewing of the Holy Spirit" (Titus 3:5).

Nor by money! Money is valuable for many things, but valueless in securing salvation. No man can buy his salvation. If he could, salvation would be a bargain, counter matter, a purchasable commodity. It would give the banker an advantage over the beggar. If such were so, salvation would be an extension of Wall Street. Such falsehood God tolerates not. "Without money and without price" (Isa. 56:1).

There is no such thin gas salvation without exception. There were two thieves on the cross. One was saved. The other lost. Jesus did not say, "Today shall YE be with me in Paradise," but he said, "Today shalt THOU be with me in Paradise" (Luke 23:43). And, besides, if God is too good to let creatures of choice be lost, what justification would God have for not sparing his own Son? "He that believeth not hath been judged already" (John 3:18). Conscious, eternal punishment is the portion of every unbeliever. "Believe on the Lord Jesus Christ, and thou shalt be saved" (Acts 16:31). "For by grace are ye saved through faith; and that not of yourselves: it is the gift of God: not of works lest any man should boast" (Ephesians 2:8-9). "Verily, verily, I say unto you, He that heareth my word, and believeth on him that sent me, hath everlasting life, and shall not come into condemnation: but is passed from death unto life" (John 5:24).

Solemn, indeed, and full of awe, the answer to the question, "What shall the end be of them that obey not the Gospel of our Lord Jesus Christ?" "And to you who are troubled rest with us, when the Lord Jesus shall be revealed from heaven with his mighty angels, in flaming fire taking vengeance on them that know not God, and obey not the Gospel of our Lord Jesus Christ; who shall be punished with everlasting destruction from the presence of the Lord, and from the glory of his power" (2 Thess. 1:7-9).

Their fate will be in the hands of him they crucified, for "he hath appointed a day, in the which he will judge the world in righteousness by that man whom he hath ordained; whereof he hath given assurance unto all men, in that he hath raised him from the dead" (Acts 17:31).

Those who refuse him as Saviour will have to stand before him as judge. Those who prefer the religion of the flesh, with the sins of the flesh and the pleasures of the flesh, and have rejected the Sacrifice will have to bear their own sins in hell—in that dreadful place where the lost, lashed by the hot breath of hell's inferno, in a storm that knows no abatement, are forever dying, yet living still—"the smoke of their torment ascending up forever" (Isa. 34:10). "He that believeth on the Son hath everlasting life: and he that believeth not the Son shall not see life; but the wrath of God abideth on him" (John 3:36).

Go teach the degraded pagan. Go teach the deluded Mohammedan. Go teach the superstitious African. Tell them all that the finished work of Jesus is the only way of acceptance with God. Go tell the polished scholar. Go tell the profound philosopher. Go tell the vaunting moralist. Tell them that the doctrine of Christ crucified is the only knowledge that can save the soul. Go tell the bold skeptic. Go tell the bold blasphemer. Go tell the polluted libertine. Preach it to the sullen murderer in the cell. Let it ring in every human heart and thrill in every human heart, till the gladness of earth shall be the counterpart of heaven.

Christ doth call us!

Listen, O man of the broken career! The marred vessel can be moulded again in beauty and grace. The broken life can be transfigured into strength and power. The tragedy can be turned to song and the darkened pathway flooded with glory. "I, even I, am he that blotteth out thy transgressions for mine own sake; and I will not remember thy sins" (Isa. 43:25). It is the voice that reached the soul of John Bunyan, the dissolute tinker, and John Newton, the blaspheming infidel, and Jerry McAuley, the Bowery criminal, and turned their blighted and broken lives into triumphant victories of redeeming power. It is the voice that called Moody, the boot-store clerk, and Rodney Smith, the gypsy lad, and John Ruskin, the apostle of art, and Henry Drummond, the cultured professor, and sent them forth to be flaming evangelists of the Kingdom of Heaven. The same voice and the same God is calling you, here and now!

Men! I care not who you are or what you are, cultured

or ignorant, moral or immoral, high or low, rich or poor. God can redeem your life from failure, and make it an everlasting success—*IF YOU WILL GIVE HIM THE CHANCE.* God can redeem your soul from sin! "He is able to save them unto the uttermost that come unto God by him" (Heb. 7: 25).

He wants to give you the best of both worlds, to make, for each of you, "life, death, and the great forever, one grand sweet song"—a triumph song of eternal redemption.

Will you let him do it? Will you cry: "Lord Jesus, here I am, sin and failure, and everything else. Take me and make me all that Thou seest I ought to be. I give Thee control now and forever."

Will you do it now? And believe he answers? And then go out to live with him? In the power and glory of the redeemed life? God grant it for Jesus sake!!!

"For Christ also hath once suffered for sins, the just for the unjust, that he might bring us to God, being put to death in the flesh."—I Peter 3: 18.

"Unto him that loved us, and washed us from our sins in his own blood, and hath made us kings and priests unto God and his Father; to him be glory and dominion for ever and ever. Amen" (Rev. 1: 5-6).

Amen!

THE RIDER OF THE WHITE HORSE

Edwin H. Byington

> *"And I saw and behold, a white horse, and he that sat thereon had a bow; and there was given unto him a crown; and he came forth conquering and to conquer."*
>
> *Revelation vi.2*

Edwin H. Byington was born at Adrianople, Turkey, in 1861. He was educated at Robert College, Constantinople and at Amherst, where he received his bachelor's degree in 1883. He studied two years at the Hartford Theological Seminary and later graduated from Auburn Seminary in 1887. He was ordained a Congregational minister the same year. The four years following he was pastor at Springfield, Mass., and from 1891 to 1900 was assistant to the late R. S. Storrs at the Church of the Pilgrims, Brooklyn. He was pastor at West Roxbury, Mass., and has been for a number of years professor of homiletics in Gordon College of Theology and Missions, Boston.

Prof. Byington is the author of several splendid books. His *The Children's Pulpit* was one of the first collections of sermons designed for preaching to children. He has also written *Open Air Preaching, A Chart of Jewish National History,* and *Pulpit Mirrors.* His *Quest For Experience in Worship* attracted widespread ·appearance last year because of the author's exceptional acquaintance with forms of worship in every part of the world.

THE RIDER OF THE WHITE HORSE

"And I saw and behold, a white horse, and he that sat thereon had a bow; and there was given unto him a crown; and he came forth conquering and to conquer."

Revelation vi.2

A white horse, a red horse, a black horse and a pale horse form one of the strange groups in the book of Revelation. The rider of the red horse seems to be war, of the black horse famine and of the pale horse death. The rider of the white horse has received a crown, carries a bow and goes forth conquering and to conquer. Nothing more definite is stated concerning him. In contrast with war, famine and death he seems to represent life—*Life's Conquering Spirit*.

Why was man created? That he might "eat, drink and be merry" and then die like the beasts of the field? Or to slave for the sovereign of the skies? Let the Bible make answer. Twice in the first chapter of Genesis God indicates his purpose in creating man:—"Let them have dominion over the fish of the sea, and over the birds of the heavens, and over the cattle and over all the earth:" "Be fruitful and multiply and replenish the earth, and subdue it; and have dominion. . . ." "Subdue the earth. Have dominion over it," was God's command to man at the very beginning. The Creator sent him forth a rider on a white horse, conquering and to conquer. Before him was spread a magnificent realm; to win it his task.

Prior to man's appearance on the earth, the animals roamed and raged, the plants multiplied in wanton confusion, gravity held everything in its relentless grasp, electricity darted in cruel destructiveness, the sea spread its threatening barriers and the winds swept all before them. The gold, the diamonds, the pearls were buried, and the coal and iron refused to come forth. Amid physical unity was a certain moral chaos. Inflexible laws operated but no reverent and reasoning creature dwelt on the earth to master and direct its manifold life.

Then was man sent to control and harmonize. This is his earthly mission, recognized long afterward when the Psalmist sang exultingly of man, "Thou makest him to have dominion over the works of thy hands. Thou hast put all things under his feet."

For thousands of years man has been riding the white horse from victory to victory. First his sovereignty consisted in gathering the fruitage of tree and vine and using the creatures for his own sustenance, but gradually he extended his control.

Most thrilling, for example, is his victory over the sea which for ages had rolled in unchallenged triumph. One day a savage on a floating log propelled it with a stick—the first boat, the first victory. Later another in a boat opened his garments, and the wind drove him—the first sail boat, the second victory. Afterwards came the memorable conquest when Columbus crossed from shore to shore, and another when the first steamboat proudly cut the waves. Great was man's exultation when the cable pierced the ocean's heart, and today its proud billows are humbled as the mysterious messages of the wireless speed on, utterly ignoring them. The waters' majestic expanse shrinks while the airplane defies as it flies from continent to continent, and all mankind watches breathlessly and bursts into applause at man's thrilling victory over the sea.

How varied his triumphs!—the rivers spanned by

countless bridges, the mountains mounted as though the iron horse had eagle wings, electricity changed from the storm king to the servant of servants. From its secret recesses, the earth, at man's demand, supplies heat, and light and power. The flowers he bids bloom in winter: he commands the plants to produce larger and richer fruitage: he tames, or cages, or banishes the animals; and now even to the fishes he says, "Live in that lake, swim in this stream, skirt these shores:" and all these obey.

Man lifting his arms in exultant prayer to the Creator might almost cry out, "At creation thou didst command us to have dominion over the earth, and to subdue all thereon. Lo, we have fulfilled thy behest."

God not only commanded man to conquer but implanted in him a passion for victory, so strong and insistent that it manifests itself not only in subduing created things but in every realm of life. How we all love to win! Why did Alexander weep? For lack of worlds to conquer; because the hunger for triumph was upon him. What did Napoleon wish? Victories. Why do our multi-millionaires seek so eagerly more money? Not because they need it, or can spend it, but because they delight in achievement. Why the widespread craving for office? The desire for dominion. Look lower, and note the brutal boxer, enduring long and exacting training and the torturing blows of his adversary. For what? Championship. Look higher, and count hundreds, perhaps thousands of scientists, observing in hospitals and experimenting in laboratories, each eager to be the conqueror of cancer.

Look about in ordinary life. The housewife strains herself to remove a little dust, high up, far back, out of sight, harmless if it stayed there a score of years; but it is a perpetual defiance, and she, born for victory, must mount and master it and scatter it to the four winds of heaven.

A man approaches his home, with quick step and buoyant bearing, with flashing eyes and radiant face; a fitting figure for the martial strains of "Lo! the conquering hero comes." Why this elation? He has just succeeded in knocking a small white ball, into some little holes with one less stroke of a stick than ever before.

So strong is this God-given delight in victory that even witnessing it in others stirs man, as in spirit they share in the conquest. The thousands in attendance at athletic contests, the astounding popularity of newspaper sporting pages, evidence a far-reaching response to the innate urge of the conquering spirit in man.

This impulse may be misdirected or even defiled. It may devote itself to the trivial instead of the ennobling; but to abjure it altogether is to lose some of manhood's glory, to disobey God who implanted it and commanded obedience to it. If a human being lacks it altogether he must be classed with the halt, the maimed, the blind.

The presence of sin on the earth did not invalidate, but rather enhanced the urge and emphasized the command. In the presence of the first recorded sin in Genesis Jehovah God said unto the tempter, "I will put enmity between thee and the woman, and between thy seed and her seed: he shall bruise thy head and thou shalt bruise his heel." What is that but the battling spirit, sent forth with crown and bow, conquering and to conquer temptation and sin?

In the moral and spiritual realm also the human race has heard the command and felt the urge to smite and win. Think of the sins once rampant, now crushed; of evils once condoned, now condemned; of crimes once common, now rare; and others still in existence that are being steadily, even if slowly, pushed back by an advancing Christian civilization. Infanticide, cannibalism, burn-

ing at the stake, crucifixion, punishment by physical tor-
ture and mutilation, slavery, human sacrifice and immor-
ality as factors in worship, withcraft and other such, once
receiving widespread sanction, are now viewed with horror. Dueling is denounced: drunkenness is despised:
lynching is abhorred: exploitation of the weak and young,
for very shame, seeks sheep's clothing to conceal its claws
and fangs. Even Mars, once claiming precedence in every
emergency, finds himself attacked as never before and begins to resist as though fighting for his very life.

Monotheism, for centuries sustaining a precarious existence on Jordan's banks has spread over continents,
permeated nations, and is driving back, and further back,
polytheism, henotheism, dualism, animism and fetichism,
and is ready to demand immediate and unconditional surrender. Man's conquering spirit has won victories in the
moral and spiritual realm rivalling those in the physical
realm; for he was born to conquer everywhere.

That we are Christians intensifies as well as purifies
this conquering spirit within us, for such was the temper
of Christ. He began his ministry by smiting temptation in
the wilderness, by flinging from the temple the desecrat-
ing traders, by putting evil spirits to flight, by o'er-
mastering disease, by subduing natural forces. Rulers
shrank from his rebukes. Behold him in Gethsemane,
binding and banishing his own fears. On the cross he
smote sin and opened a way of escape for its captives.
Into the domain of death he went, riding a white horse,
conquering and to conquer; and in his resurrection he
emerged a victor, having won the strategic battle which
led the apostle to cry out, "For he must reign till he hath
put all his enemies under his feet. The last enemy that
shall be abolished is death."

Every Christian, like his leader, should be mounted on

a white horse. Our Christian faith should arouse within us resolution as well as resignation, hunger for victory as well as humility, a masterful temper as well as a submissive spirit. We are warriors, not simply wards of a sheltering Providence. Each has a bow, and should shoot straight and strong. A crown has been given, and for it a kingdom must be won. To guide our higher powers, to check our baser passions, to bind the sin that doth so easily beset us, to eradicate evils from the community, to make the kingdoms of this world subject to the Lord Christ—to this end did we have our first birth, and to this end were we born again.

What! call ourselves crowned conquerors! How dare we, while that evil habit we have striven to break, still retains a hold on us? Unable to drive wayward thoughts out of our minds, can we expect the thrill of triumph? How often have our daily tasks, even the simplest and the easiest, proved pitiful failures and in our larger aims we have drawn the bow but to miss the mark. Sometimes at the close of an unfortunate day, when everything has gone wrong, the whole head is sick and the whole heart faint. What then? Then, O Christian, though prostrate in the dust, trampled under foot, crushed—look up. Beside you stands a white horse, your horse. Rise, mount him, and again on to the fray, and as you go, say:—

"All I have toiled to do has been done ill;
All I have striven to grasp escaped me still;
The battle is unwon, though close the night,
Yet still I've fought, though sometimes weak the fight.
Though I have failed, in naught do I complain,
All that I ask is leave to fight again."

And then ride on in the conquering spirit which God gave you when he created you, and which Christ bestowed upon you when he redeemed you.

What is true of the individual Christian is equally applicable to the Church. Thrilling was the great commission God gave man as he completed the work of creation, "Subdue The Earth;" but even more amazing was the greater commission Christ gave his followers as he completed the work of redemption, "Disciple All Nations."

At Pentecost the conquering spirit took possession of the Christian Church. Behold "the boldness of Peter and John," listen to the defiant and triumphant Stephen. Glorious the Pauline interpretation of the Gospel, and precious his practical maxims for daily living, but of what avail these had not the conquering spirit animated and sustained him?—a spirit never diverted by threatening perils on land and sea, unflinchingly facing Jewish and Roman persecutions, undismayed by the treacherous hostility of Judaizing leaders, and undiminished by the fickleness and folly of Christian converts. What profit is there if the Church holds Pauline doctrines, and practices Pauline ethics but lacks the Pauline conquering spirit?

For three centuries this spirit characterized the Church. Taken literally, the saying, "The blood of the martyrs is the seed of the Church" is utterly untrue. Romans moved thus at the sight of blood? How absurd! Slaves' blood flowed freely, daily, and slaves outnumbered freemen, sometimes ten to one. The crucifixion of criminals they often saw. Demure maidens and stately matrons, with the multitude, sought the ampitheater, eager to see blood flow, caring little whether they watched trained warriors, or cringing captives, or slaves, or accused men and women, or wild beasts. They revelled in such spectacles and the blood of the martyrs anywhere only added one thrill of enjoyment. What was it that did stir them? Pity? No. It was the conquering spirit of the martyrs. This became the seed of the Church. They went to death with a triumphant bearing, as men march to victory. They prayed with a confident faith. They sang exultingly. Their absolute assurance of ultimate triumph applied not only to themselves but also to their cause and their king. As Pilate, marvelling greatly at Jesus, exclaimed "Art thou a King then?" so many a Roman, beholding a Christian martyr, exclaimed in his heart, "Art thou a conqueror then?" and himself was conquered for Christ.

When Constantine first tolerated, then patronized and finally accepted Christianity, and when it became the established religion of the Roman Empire, the urge of the conquering spirit naturally diminished but did not altogether disappear. No heroic horsemen ever rode the white horse with greater skill and success than the missionaries of the middle ages. Ulfilas, though defective his Gospel and inadequate his efforts, wrought gloriously among the Goths with an influence reaching other Barbarian tribes, so that when they swept over the Roman Empire from the North they were no such scourge as the Moslems from the South. He had given to them the Bible in their own tongue. He had held before them the cross. Patrick's triumphant establishment of Christianity in Ireland has been overshadowed by the silly story of his driving the snakes out of the island. A boy slave, carried into Ireland, he escaped and vowed a vow that he would return and conquer his captors, by winning them to Christ. And he did. Boniface, defeated in his early missionary efforts among the Friesians, later won Germany for Christ, and became bishop and archbishop. Then he gave up all his ecclesiastical positions and returned in one more effort to win the Friesians. By them he was slain, but he was slain riding a white horse. What shall be said of those other horsemen?—Cyril and Methodius, seeking the Slavs; Augustine riding into England, Columba into Scot-

THE RIDER OF THE WHITE HORSE   173

land, Ansgar into Scandinavia. Or if, passing out of the
ranks of the missionaries, we look at Gregory the Great,
St. Francis, Waldo, Wycliff, Huss, Luther, Zwingli, Calvin and Knox, we realize that the conquering spirit had
not vanished from the life of the church.

Is this all there is to the picture? No. Sometimes in the
past centuries the beholder would have looked in vain
for the white horse and his rider. He was not on the field
of battle. Perhaps he had turned in retreat and had fled
in fear. Perhaps he had galloped off on a private venture
for fame and worldly power. Sometimes the rider had
dismounted, that he might gather booty, caring more for
wealth than spiritual victory, or that he might indulge
himself in ease, and luxury, and dissipation; or that he
might bargain with the enemy, and win, by surrendering,
a kingdom of this world more to his taste. The sad fact is
that too often the Christian Church has not been riding
the white horse, but with bow unstrung, and crown
pawned for a paltry price, has left the horse to roam
undirected.

One hundred and fifty years ago, about the time of the
American Revolution and the French Revolution, the
rider of the white horse seemed to have vanished. Then,
in the early part of the nineteenth century, he reappeared
with the Church in the saddle. What a conquering spirit pre-
vailed! What victories were won! The work of missions
was revived and missionary societies of all sorts, including
a great number of Bible Societies, were multiplied. Sunday Schools sprang up on all sides, with a friendly rivalry
as to which was first. Evangelism swept in waves. Schools
of theology were established, religious journalism was
born, and such social evils as slavery were assailed.

During the past few decades, however, the white horse
and his rider have again been less in evidence, while the

other three have been in the foreground. Most conspic-
uous has been the red horse of war. Militarism became
more and more rampant, culminating in the World War.
Even now its consequences loom large, while some are
carefully grooming the red horse for possible future service. The black horse of famine has been trampling under
foot many cherished beliefs which had sufficed for the
spiritual sustenance of generations. He would render
meaningless and useless the incarnation, the redemption
by the cross, the resurrection, even assaulting the freedom
of the will, the reality of morality, the existence of the
soul and the personality of God. Many are famishing.
They ask for bread and receive a stone. The pale horse
of death also has been destroying, seeking to obliterate
moral restraints, ethical standards, habits of obedience,
modesty and reverence, even invading the home and de-
claring the doom of organized Christianity.

All this has resulted in a mood not unlike that pre-
vailing one hundred and fifty years ago. A kind of hope-
lessness has crept into the church. It seems to have lost
the conquering spirit. Many love it as a lost cause and
secretly weave flags of truce for the hour of need. Every
critic seems a Goliath, with no shepherd lad in sight. It is
suffering from an inferiority complex, and is ready to
surrender any habit, any belief, any possession that is
challenged. Worse than that, it seems sometimes psycho-
pathic. How it loves to think and talk about its ailments!
Wrapt attention has he been receiving, and even applause,
who pointed out declining church attendance, lack of missionary interest, the dissatisfaction of youth with its program, the indifference of the masses, the powerlessness of
the pulpit. For some years it has been "enjoying poor
health," morbidly brooding over its failures, accounting
each a serious symptom, perhaps to be fatal.

The church has been in this mood before, but never for long. At heart it knows that it was born to conquer; that a confident courage, a triumphant temper, even an audacious heroism should permeate and animate its ranks. Its mood just now seems to be changing. It is growing somewhat weary of Jeremiads; agnosticism is getting tiresome, and criticism stale. Searching for the "irreducible minimum" of the Gospel and everything else seems less fascinating; stripping Jesus of all but a bare humanity is not proving soul-satisfying: it begins to feel that it would like to turn from revelling in negations to rejoicing in affirmations.

It is time for the rider of the white horse to resume the leading position he had originally. The hour has come for a restoration of the conquering spirit, with a firm grasp on the great vital truths of Christianity, with a fearless proclamation of strong convictions, with a resolute determination to evangelize the world, with an unflinching purpose to banish war and social injustice, to put to flight prejudices and errors, and to smite the debasing influences that surround and assail youth. For such tasks dauntless courage should be hailed as king of the Christian virtues, a courage not so much daring to deny as daring to affirm, not so much brave to belittle as brave to believe great truths, entering the lists not as the color-bearer of doubt but as the champion of faith, fashioning strong convictions into keen weapons, with a spirit that anticipates not defeat but victory. Such is the purpose and temper of the rider of the white horse.

Whence cometh such optimism? Not from mere physical buoyancy or temperamental hopefulness: not from statistics juggled to cheer us or an array of arguments; but from a vision of him who later in the book of Revelation is pictured as riding on a white horse followed by the armies of heaven, also on white horses. His name is "Faithful and True," "The Word of God," "King of Kings and Lord of Lords," even our Christ, the Eternal Christ. Pertinent and profitable is the cry "Back to Christ;" but "Forward with Christ" is needed for the creation of the conquering spirit. That spirit springs from conscious contact with the ever-living, ever-present Christ. He said, when he gave the command to win the nations, "Lo, I am with you always even unto the end of the world." So he speaks to us now.

Study the lives of Christianity's triumphant horsemen and you will find that they were all conscious of riding behind a great leader. They were following not a memory but a living and conquering Master, of whose ultimate triumph they had not a shadow of doubt. Eventually every knee would bow and every tongue would confess that Jesus Christ is Lord to the glory of God the Father. Eventually the kingdoms of this world would be the kingdom of their Lord Christ. Eventually righteousness would cover the earth as the waters cover the seas. Thus today let the Church leap into the saddle, place upon its forehead the crown, grasp the bow and ride on, confident with a conquering spirit as it follows its leader, also riding a white horse.

WHERE OUR GREATEST BATTLES ARE FOUGHT

J. H. JOWETT

"Men ought always to pray and not to faint."
Luke xviii.1

The late J. H. Jowett was born at Halifax, England, in 1864.
He was educated in the University of Edinburgh, receiving his
M.A. degree in 1887, and in Oxford University, where he
studied from 1887 to 1890. In this same year he was ordained
a Congregational minister. His career was marked by long and
fruitful pastorates. From 1895 to 1911 he was pastor of Carr's
Lane Church, Birmingham. In 1911 he came to the Fifth
Avenue Presbyterian Church, New York, where he remained
until his return to England in 1918 to assume the pastorate
of Westminister Chapel, London. This pastorate he held until
the time of his death.

The sermon, "Where Our Greatest Battles Are Fought",
was preached during his ministry at Westminister. It appeared
in his volume *God—Our Contemporary*. In all his writing is
to be found a distinguishing brawn of thought and delicacy
of expression. Other books from his pen include *Apostolic
Optimism, Things That Matter Most, The Passion For Souls,
The Transfigured Church, The Whole Armour of God, and
The High Calling.*

WHERE OUR GREATEST BATTLES ARE FOUGHT

"Men ought always to pray and not to faint."
Luke xviii.1

That word was spoken when the Master's noon-tide
was already past. The shadows were lengthening upon the
way, and some of the Lord's sayings breathed the air of
coming night. The road was heavy with deepening gloom,
and now and again in the windings one caught the glimpse
of a cross. The disciples were startled into confusion. The
happenings ran athwart all their expectations. The things
which the Master was speaking about were a brutal defiance of their fondest hopes. They had been looking for
a golden harvest, and now the snow was falling. They
had been eagerly anticipating the gaily coloured dignities
of dominion, and their eyes were now turned upon the
black trappings of defeat. They had been stepping forward to a kingdom, and to the shared sovereignties of a
throne, and now a scaffold begins to loom at the end of
the road. And so their minds were all at sixes and sevens.
They were torn with uncertainties. They were distracted
with doubt. Fear, too, came into their hearts with chilling
menace. And some of them were tempted to retreat.
Others became weary and heavy in their goings. Others
again began to faint.

And in our Scriptural passage we have one of the Lord's
specifics which is to be used against the assault of circumstances, and the threat of impending doom. What is this
specific which makes one master of the changing way?

"Men ought always to pray and not to faint." The guiding word may mean that men are always to pray and never to faint in prayer. Or it may mean that men ought always to pray and they would never faint even when antagonisms rear themselves like awful mountain ranges between them and their goal. It is probable that both interpretations are equally true and that both are included in the Master's mind and purpose. For the cardinal matter is this: the heavy emphasis which Jesus Christ puts upon the ministry of prayer as a predominant means of grace. "Men ought *always* to pray." The fellowship is to run through all the changing seasons of life, through spring and summer, and autumn and winter. "Always to pray!" In the springtime of life, when the blossoms are forming, in the winter when the snow is falling and the trees are bare! When we are sauntering through the green pastures or toiling across the wilderness! In the playfield or in the battlefield! In the winsome dawn which sheds its light upon the marriage altar, or in the empty darkness which gathers about the tomb. "Men ought *always* to pray." Such is the fervent pressure of the Master's word. And what He urged others to do He was always doing Himself. He prayed always. He prayed in the brilliant sunshine when the multitude would have taken Him by force and made Him a king. He prayed in the night in which He was betrayed,—when all others had fled. He prayed in the open fields when He was feeding a famished crowd. He prayed by the grave of Lazarus. He prayed in the midst of the pestilence that walketh in darkness; He prayed in the midst of the destruction which wasteth at noon-day. Most surely He exemplified the counsel which He gave to His disciples when He said that "Men ought always to pray."

Now let us consider one or two primary matters concerning this mighty business of prayer. And let us say first of all that the ministry of prayer is not entirely one with the exercise of petition. Prayer and petition are not synonyms, two names for the same thing. If the realm of prayer finds its symbol in some noble estate, then petition is like one field on the landscape. And there are seasons of prayer when we need not be in that particular field at all. Our spirit may be wandering in other parts of the wide domain. I am not disparaging the mighty prerogative of petition. But I am saying that it is only a part of our spiritual inheritance.

> Thou art coming to a King,
> Large petitions with thee bring.

Yes, I know it, and there are seasons when I would come to the King, burdened with intercessions, and I would spread the world of my necessities before the favour of His grace. I am coming to a King, but I am coming to more than a King. I am coming to a Father, and Fatherhood is larger than Kinghood, just as home is larger than a throne. A king may have gifts at his disposal, he may have honours and benefits and offices to confer upon his subjects; but fatherhood moves in a circle of intimacies and shared secrets, even in the matchless commerce of truth and grace and love. When prayer turns into this marvellous realm it is not so much a suppliant, laden with petition, as a wondering child walking in the revealing companionship of the Father in heaven. Prayer is not always like Lazarus, clothed in rags, and bowing in suppliancy at the rich man's gate; it is sometimes like Lazarus in the Father's bosom, dwelling in the secret place of the most High, and walking and talking in the shadow of the Almighty.

I may be pardoned for dwelling upon this distinction,

as I think we are not always conscious of the range of the inheritance of the saints in light, and we only occupy a corner in our Father's house. I was once present at a prayer meeting, and one led us in prayer who was very evidently a disciplined traveller in the realms of grace. He left the field of petition, and he went wanderingly and wonderingly along among the unsearchable riches of Christ as though he were straying among the amazing glories of matchless woods. And the leader of the meeting bore with the traveller for some time and then broke out impatiently, "Brother, ask God for something! Ask God for something!" But the brother did not seem to have anything to ask for just then; it was quite enough to be walking with his Father in the boundless realms of grace. "Ask God for something!" No, prayer is not always petition, sometimes it is just communion. It is the exquisite ministry of friendship. It is the delicate passage of intimacies; it is the fellowship of the Holy Ghost.

Now let me state a second primary matter concerning this mighty business of prayer. If it is not always in the form of petition neither need it be always in the form of words. I want to try to say something which is very real to me, but which almost refuses the clumsy ministry of expression. There is a very vital part of prayer which can do without the vehicle of words. We can escape from the burden of the limitation of words. Who has not felt the bondage of speech, the cumbersomeness of words when he has sought to pray? And who has not experienced the peril of living words becoming dead forms? The lithe, nervous, blood-filled words have stiffened into corpses, and all our prayer has been dead. How often it happens that we do not possess our words; we are not their owners. They are not our children, coursing with hot blood which has been gathered at the springs of our own life. How often our words have no vital communion with us, and when we are not their owners we become their slaves. So there are times in prayer when I long to escape from the ministries of words, and to have wordless fellowship in the Presence of God.

This is what I mean. First of all, we quietly and reverently put ourselves into the Presence of God, we collect our scattered consciousness in the sense that God is near, and we come before His Presence. How is the Presence revealed? Who can say? Are there any means or methods which men and women have practised in the realization of the Presence of the unseen Friend? Yes there are, but I suppose we must say that there are almost as many ways as there are people who have practised them. Some call in the aid of a devout imagination, and in the secret place they realize a face, even the face which was unveiled to us in the Nazarene. To others the sacred Presence assumes no form, because there is no image which their consecrated imagination can frame which seems worthy of their unutterable devotion. Horace Bushnell led his spirit into a certain bright luminousness in which the Presence of the Lord was veiled, and he communed with Him in the light. That is also the way of a very dear friend of mine who is greatly learned in the things of grace. His spirit withdraws in the Presence of a shining splendour, and there he holds his fellowship. Others have nothing of this kind at all. They just recall themselves into God's Presence and without any image of form or any sense of light they know and feel that God is near. But these differences do not really matter, and it is well for everyone just to take the way which gives them the most intimate assurance of the Presence of God. Here is one soul about whom I have recently been reading.

"Well, as I was saying, when we got to the woods,

Mercy stayed in a little grass path by the edge, and opened a very dull-looking book, and I went into the wood alone. At first it was awfully thick and tangled, and all alive with little winged and feathered things that darted off quickly or rose with a whirr. I love that, don't you— all the stirring of bunnies and dickie birds in a wood? Then I got to a little clearing and sat down on a fallen tree in the sunshine. The sky was blue, blue, the kind of blue that goes on for ever, and the little shadow of leaves all lacy on the grass. It was just Beauty, and nothing else —almost better than music! Then, as I looked at the intense blue of the sky, I changed, from knowing Beauty, to knowing Love. Of course, I can't begin to tell you, but I felt I was in the presence of God. He was around me like light, like showers of light, and like love. I wanted to kneel, but I could not move. I could not think at all for a minute—'a minute,'—I don't know, it might have been a second or an hour, for all I know. Then my mind said, 'This is Life.' Now I know."

But I think it is not necessary for us to emphasize anyone's particular way as being the way for others. Never mind another's way, seek your own. Recall your spirit into the silence. You may not necessarily be in solitude; it may even be in the midst of a crowded train. Withdraw into the secret depths of your own spirit. Quietly say to yourself that the Eternal God is near who revealed Himself in Jesus Christ our Lord. You may be perfectly sure that you will become more expert in this sense of discernment as you continue in its practice. You will realize that you are in the Presence of God. And now, as you realize it, introduce in that Presence anything which concerns you and in which you have a vital interest. Let your imagination rest on that thing, and quietly bring it to the sacred silence where you are closeted with God.

See it clearly, and then, with great deliberateness, introduce it almost visibly into the sacred Presence. That is to say you are now intelligently and imaginatively bringing some interest into the heavenly places, and you are setting it in the light of God. That is again to say, you are thinking of something while your mind is suffused with the sense of God. You are bringing the two into fellowship, you are setting them face to face. You need not utter a word, you can escape from the crude bondage of your own ignorance, and from the narrow limitations of speech. You offer no verbal petition, but you set your human concern in the mighty and pervasive influence of the Spirit of God. There must be no irreverent haste. There must be no frivolous tramping of the holy courts. It must all be done with patient deliberateness, steadily holding the interest, whatever it be, in the holy light of God. And no words are needful.

Suppose the vital interest be your own child. Well, then, set yourself in the sacred silence, with a sense that you are near your Lord, and then, with alert imagination, bring your child into the holy place. See him there, hold him there. And what are you doing? You are establishing vital currencies between him and the divine Presence, and you can do it without the ministry of words. Of course, you may speak if you will, but I think your words will be few. For in setting him there in the silence you are praying, and you are presenting him to the grace and wisdom of God, and your dedicated homage is providing channels for the river of the water of life.

Or it may be some personal habit which constitutes your vital concern. Or it may be some particular piece of business. It may be some loss which you have suffered, or some great gain which you have made. It may be a bride. It may be a widow. It may be an orphan. It may be a people, a race or a tribe. It may be one of ten thousand things. I am urging you to practice this means of grace, in thus introducing our interests to the sacred Presence of the Almighty. See them there, and hold them there, and whether it be with words or without words, whether in verbal devotion or in attitude and act, you are carrying out something of the Master's counsel when He said, "Men ought always"—in everything and everywhere—"to pray and not to faint."

Well now, it is in the field of prayer that life's critical battles are lost or won. We must conquer all our circumstances there. We must first of all bring them there. We must survey them there. We must master them there. In prayer we bring our spiritual enemies in the Presence of God and we fight them there. Have you tried that? Or have you been satisfied to meet and fight your foes in the open spaces of the world? If I am like Bunyan's pilgrim, and encounter Apollyon on the exposed road, and begin my warfare there I shall be sadly beaten, and he will leave me bruised and broken by the way. My resource is immediately to get him into the field of prayer and engage him there. The struggle was going against Bunyan's pilgrim until he changed the manner of his fighting.

"Apollyon as fast made at him, throwing darts as thick as hail; by the which, notwithstanding all that Christian could do to avoid it, Apollyon wounded him in his head, his hand, and foot. This made Christian give a little back; Apollyon, therefore, followed his work again, and Christian again took courage, and resisted as manfully as he could. This sore combat lasted for above half a day, even till Christian was almost quite spent; for you must know that Christian, by reason of his wounds, must needs grow weaker and weaker.

"Then Apollyon, espying his opportunity, began to gather up close to Christian, and, wrestling with him, gave him a dreadful fall; and with that Christian's sword flew out of his hand. Then said Apollyon, 'I am sure of thee now.' And with that he had almost pressed him to death, so that Christian began to despair of life. But, as God would have it, while Apollyon was fetching his last blow, whereby to make a full end of this good man, Christian nimbly reached out his hand for his sword, and caught it, saying, 'rejoice not against me, O mine enemy; when I fall I shall arise,' and with that gave him a deadly thrust, which made him give back, as one that has received his mortal wound. Christian, perceiving that, made at him again, saying, 'Nay, in all these things we are more than conquerors through Him that loved us.' "

I am, therefore, trying to say in the spiritual realm what Lord Fisher once said in the realm of material warfare. He said, "Compel your enemy to fight you on your own drill ground." Yes, indeed, and when we fight the world, and the flesh and the devil on the drill ground of prayer, we have a certain victory. Let us bring our evil thoughts on to the field of prayer. Let us drag our mean judgments on to the field of prayer. Let us drive our ignoble purpose on to the same field, and our insane prejudices, and our malicious practices, and our tyrannical passions. Let us fight them on our own drill ground and slay them there. Men ought always to bring their evil antagonisms and besetments into the Presence of God. Force them into God's holy place and there fight and slay. Men ought always to pray, and they will not faint in the heaviest day.

And on the same field of prayer we must bring our troubles, for we get on to the top of them in the holy place. It very frequently happens that many of our troubles lose their fictitious stature when we bring them into the Presence of the eternal God. They shrink when we set them in a large place. It is almost amusing how little things appear big when they are set in confined and narrow spaces. Put them in a bigger field and they lose their alarming size. And there is many an anxiety that looks gigantic until we set it in the holy field of prayer in the Presence of the Lord. Aye, and there are other things which seem enormous and overwhelming until we set them in infinite relations. Sometimes a grave seems so big that it appears to fill the world. There is nothing in the world but the grave. When we see it on the fields of communion and in the glory of the light of the risen Lord, captivity is led captive, as death itself is buried in the eternal life of God. It is not our father's purpose that we should see our dead in cemeteries, but rather in the heavenly fields of the infinite love; and it is there that death loses its cold and cruel servitude. It is when we compel death to go with us on to the fields of divine communion that the grave is seen to be only a vestibule of the life indeed. "O death, where is thy sting?" "O grave, where is thy victory?"

And even when some of our troubles remain, as indeed they will, it is on the fields of prayer that we get above them, and assume and assert our sovereignty in the power of the risen Lord. We have a very familiar phrase which, I think, is very suggestive. We say, "Under the circumstances!" But why should we be under them? Why should we not be regnant above them? Why slaves and not masters? Why under and not above? It is on the field of prayer that we get our circumstances beneath our feet. "Thou shalt tread upon the lion and the adder, the young lion and the dragon shalt thou trample under feet." "Ye shall have power to tread on serpents." "I keep under

my body and bring it into subjection." That is the pur-
posed sovereignty which is ours in Christ. And we daily
assume the sovereignty and we ride our enemies on the
wonder-working fields of prayer. Said Lord Fisher, "Fight
your enemy on your own drill ground." Very well, then,
lead your troubles on to those holy fields, and get above
them in the emancipating grace of the Lord.

But prayer has larger relationships than any of these.
I can not only bring my spiritual enemies on to the battle
field of prayer and slay them there. And I can not only
bring my troubles into the expansive realm of prayer and
ride them as the Creator rides the storm. I can bring the
burdens and necessities of humanity into the sacred Presence, and in my own life I can become a point of vital
contact between God and the human race. For I am not a
unit of mankind, isolated and independent, a being of separated interests, self-centered and self-contained. I am
just a fraction, a single member, a limb, a mere fragment
of humanity, and I am indissolubly connected with it.
The solidarity of the human race is inclusive of me, and
I am a vital and indivisible part. The moral and spiritual
blood of the race runs through me, and through me it cir-
culates throughout humanity. When, therefore, I com-
mune with God in prayer I become a point of contact, an
inlet through which the divine life flows into the veins
and arteries of humanity. That is no idle figure of speech.
Every man is an inlet through which clean or unclean
energies pour into the general life-pool of the human race.
We cannot help it. My points of contact determine the
character of my contributions, and if my supreme contact is with God in the communion of prayer, I become
an open channel through which the blessed influences flow
into human fellowship for its eternal good. And so the
prayer-ground is the common ground of racial enrich-

ment. The hands that make contact with the battery direct the electrical dynamic to every fibre and tissue of the body. And hands that are uplifted in prayer are conductors of the divine dynamic to the general brotherhood of humanity. And therefore our Master counsels us to retire into the secret place. Create a sensitive quietness about your spirit. Realize the sacred Presence. And then slowly and deliberately, in the holy place, present your helpmeets and your antagonisms, your privileges and your necessities, your banes and your pains, your laughter and your tears. And in your life the ancient miracle of grace shall again be wrought, for the Son of Righteousness shall arise upon you with healing in His wings.

GUARDIANS OF THE GLEAM—AND THE GLOW

Gaius Glenn Atkins

> *"And be not transformed to this world: but be transformed by the renewing of your mind, that ye may prove what is that good, and acceptable, and perfect will of God."*
>
> *Romans xxi.2*

The selection of Gaius Glenn Atkin's new book, *PROCES-SION OF THE GODS*, as the first choice of the Religious Book Club for October, 1930, is evidence of the respect in which his work as a writer and thinker is held. He did his undergraduate work in Ohio State University, and was graduated in 1888; he studied law in the Cincinnati Law School and received his LL.B. degree from that institution in 1891. For the next three years he taught history, then went to Yale and took up the study of theology. He was ordained into the Congregational ministry in 1895. In 1906 Dartmouth conferred upon him the degree of Doctor of Divinity. The University of Vermont conferred this same degree upon him in 1904 and in 1923 gave him the degree of L.H.D.

Dr. Atkins held several Eastern pastorates. He was twice pastor of the First Congregational Church, Detroit, serving fourteen years in all in that Church. In 1927 he was made Hoyt Professor of sociology and homiletics at Auburn Theological Seminary. He is the author of a number of books, including *The Making of the Christian Mind*, *Modern Religious Cults* and *Movements*, and *Pilgrims of the Lonely Road*.

GUARDIANS OF THE GLEAM—AND
THE GLOW

*"And be not transformed to this world: but
be transformed by the renewing of your mind,
that ye may prove what is that good, and acceptable, and perfect will of God."*

Romans xxi.2

What Paul actually asked of the Roman Christians
was that they should be "boiling" in spirit—an entirely
desirable attitude provided the conditions warrant it.
But even "boiling" saints are hard to live with and a vast
deal of the business of life can not be carried on helpfully
in a state of superheated effervescence—besides how can
one be quite sure that it is a purely spiritual boiling? Life
asks something more constant than that—a spirit whose
intensities have in them some steadfastness of light and
warmth caught from far and unfailing sources. Moffatt
has done more than find a fresh and suggestive rendering
for a time-worn phrase, he has reached the heart of life's
greatest need and revealed its rarest possibilities when
he caught and fixed the content of the Apostle's imperative: "Maintain the spiritual glow."

The twelfth chapter of Romans is the most demanding
chapter St. Paul ever wrote. His successive clauses are
like the staccato of a trip hammer; they are forging the
framework of the ethical structure of Christianity. In
sovereign imperatives a handful of unconsidered folk in
Rome are summoned to escape the world, be recast in
heavenly molds, renew their minds, bless the power that
persecuted them, return good for evil, subdue the enor-

mous and alien power of the world by their patience and confound it by their goodness and win it by their love. And just at the heart of a mandate like that he sets this arresting condition of it all—the one quality without which all the rest are strangely incomplete.

He should, one would think, have suggested methods of organization and mobilized definite and driving powers adequate in the concrete solidity to the weight they were to carry. He asks instead a state of the soul elusive as the play of firelight in a shadowed room for which his translators have hitherto found no adequate rendering and which, when the right word is found, belongs to the realm of the poet rather than the moralist.

I

The dictionary does not help us much here. How can you fence off a word like that with a definition? The fire on our hearthstones, the light in the western sky, the inner echoes of noble music, the nobler states of our own souls are better definitions of glow and gleam than any dictionary. In the world without, any glow is a subdued constancy of light, a witness to tenacious fires which have reached the heart of the fuel they burn and add to even heat a mellow radiance. In our own spirits any glow is happy exaltation. It is response to beauty and nobility— the awe with which we contemplate the stars, what poetry may kindle or art evoke. It reflects sunsets and waters spread with light, lifts us up to the level of great deeds, warms our friendships and gives to love its final benediction. All things suffer a change beneath the touch of it; it has a secret power to forbid weariness, make hard things easy, summon our last hidden strength and add to life a light whose rising is from beyond the hills of time.

We drove on an unforgettable day last April through the Catskill Mountains by valley roads whose contours had been traced by rivers which sang as they labored. They sang for us again their ancient music. The forests which lay like clouds on the mountain sides were already quick with vernal force though only a thickening of buds in the tops of them acknowledged their mounting sap, a wash of green touched upland meadows with hope, fugitive bird songs made the silence lyric, a brooding, sunlit peace possessed it all. As the day passed, the high lights left the valleys, the shadows fell across our road, the waters darkened and we drove through an unsunned chill, but the sunlight lingered on the mountain tops and no twilight could utterly possess the valleys as long as we could lift up our eyes to hills which held the glow. We treasured that retreating splendor, comrades of the day, until it fled from the mountain tops to the sky; we treasured it until the hills themselves shut out the sky. Then the night fell.

Life is like that. When the glow is gone the shadows are sovereign and all the roads of it are lonely. The glow is, I say, what you please, it is always something to touch and transform a task, a relationship or an experience. It is the eagerness with which youth approaches the untested, a quality of hope to invest untravelled roads with allure and build castles of dreams beyond uncrossed horizons. It is the spirit in which we approach the consummation of some long held purpose, the light on the course our craft take as they sail into unvoyaged seas. It is the overtone of all great music, the spirit's response to the Eroica Symphony. The bride carries it across the threshold of her new home. It is what love gives to any relationship. It is tranquil happiness in assured well-being. It is ardent happiness in some unusual felicity.

It is a quality to transform the difficult and nerve us to high adventure. Byrd took it with him into his planes tuned for audacious flight. We carry it into the hazards of life when we face them freely and bravely for it is the ultimate reinforcement. The psychologist may undo it as the physicist undoes light. No matter, when the glow is gone something has gone out of life without which its tasks are weariness and its destiny so deep in shadow that we lose heart to go on. The challenge to maintain it is one of the most commanding challenges we face, the art of maintaining it the finest of arts and whatever keeps it alive is the indispensable servant of the needs of the soul. No wonder St. Paul put the injunction to maintain it as the very heart of his great chapter.

II

For the "glow" is not easy to maintain. It is at the mercy of so many chances and, beyond the mischances of life, it has to battle—the word is justly chosen—against the cumulative force of experience itself. The years themselves darken the glow of youth. No one of us can carry undimmed the eager sense of life's wonder and possibility with which we set out. There is an inevitable recession of physical force—if of nothing else—which touches with grey what once shone with glory. The horizons which seemed to hold such radiant possibilities retreat before us, or else if one reach them nothing we find has quite the quality we dreamed lay hidden there. Deepening experience brings deepening disillusionment. Routine robs the most creative vocation of that margin of the unachieved, which is the source of all high creative impulse.

Even Rembrandt's touch grows sad and Michelangelo's great figures are haunted with weariness. Morning hopes are drunk up like morning dews by the actualities of action, they seem too often to remain only as heat mirage, shifting shapes of broken dreams. Love is subject to necessities which seem to take little account of the romance of it. It is tried by temper and temperament, it is subject to economic necessity, it must bear children and labor for their need and spend itself for ends whose issues lie beyond its knowledge and acknowledge the mastery of time and change. The most engaging professions become only a way of making a living, the more wearing and less illumined tasks become the grey routine of the sequent days. How shall a man always lay brick with a glow or discover a transforming light across the furrows he turns?

Something of all this attaches to enterprises vaster than the concerns of the individual. History itself becomes the record of epochs whose persuasion of boundless possibility darkens into disillusion and whose singing voices are muted. The light fades from the templed heights of the Acropolis and the Seven Hills of Rome. The glow escapes cultures and civilizations. We ourselves are living in a time like that. The analytically despondent gravely discuss the decay of western civilization. The assertion of noble hopes to which our fathers kindled finds no contemporaneous voice. The world has grown old in a generation. Its cynicism, its disregard of spiritual values, its excessive concern for "prosperity" and the fear which haunts it are aspects of one dis-ease. The glow is dimmed. It is easy to over-write all this. I would not forget the lights which still illumine us, or assume an order in which the glow is entirely gone from the individual conduct of life or the common enterprises of our civilization. I only say that the gleam and glow are hard to maintain.

And yet if we do not maintain them the sustaining glory of life is lost. A gleamless task is heartbreaking when it is not back breaking. Something of this over-light must be caught and held if we are to go on with any force or gladness. When the preacher has lost it his sermons are arid wastes. When the worker has lost it his toil is a fretful spending of strength. When the statesman has lost it his words have no power to stir a nation and his policies become the sterile shrewdness of the politician. When the poet has lost it the music is gone from his song. When duty has lost it its paths become flinty. When love has lost it its wings are broken. When life has lost it, it is only Carlyle's little gleams of time between two eternities and the mystery of the encompassing eternities darkens the gleam. How can we go on unless some sense of well-being and well-doing makes a light and a music for us, some unspent enthusiasm informs every task and the power of the spirit to subdue to its own radiant ends even the most trying material of life asserts itself and victoriously? I tell you the task of maintaining the glow is central in life as it is in this great chapter of St. Paul.

III

How then can we maintain the spiritual glow? St. Paul did not make an imperative of an impossibility, the maintenance of it lies within the region of the will. I suppose we should begin by saying: "I *will* not let my enthusiasms grow cold, I *will* keep some feeling for my work and not let myself turn into a disillusioned and cynical machine. I *will* not let routine blind me to the meanings of life. I *will* keep something to look up to which has beauty and wonder in it." This is a creaking kind of resolution but at least it establishes the duty of maintaining the glow among the other duties of life. After that one seeks the technique of it for resolution is not enough. The best will in the world will not make life a glowing affair unless one find the art of it—and the fires to feed it.

Now there is actually among us a far greater attention to the lesser half of St. Paul's injunction than is commonly supposed. We use every device to maintain some kind of glow—cosmetics to simulate the physical glow of youth, narcotics to release us from grey monotony, an excess of restless action to stimulate jaded interest, an unbelievable variety of device to furnish substitutes for that inner sense of well-being which is fed from deep and inexhaustible springs.

There is a proper kinship between the speech of the street and the soul of the street which gives current phrases an arresting veracity. Our own time has its equivalent of the Apostle's phrase—we are "out" to get a "kick" from life. The difference between a "glow" and a "kick" is the difference between the hearthstone and the hotel foyer, between jazz and Beethoven's Ninth Symphony, between the level lights of sunset across the hills and the spotlight. Even religion forgets its inheritance and seeks its satisfactions in the same hysterical regions. But St. Paul never said "Maintain the spiritual 'kick.' "

Note the word maintain. The Apostle had in mind the glory of expectation, the sense of election and destiny which fed the zeal of apostolic Christianity. The folk of the church in Rome believed themselves children of God for whom the world had been waiting. Their redemption has been purchased by the Cross of Christ. They were heralds of a millennial dawn and the glory which played about the standards of the Imperial Legions was colorless compared with the splendor of their estate. They had, though they did not know it yet, the task of keeping that fire of the soul alive in an order which would use its terrible power to try to put it out.

In a vaster sense life itself has of its own nature a glory which makes every other flame colorless. The sources from which it is kindled are altars of mystery. It raises the forces by which the stars are fed to its own height of beauty and reality. It is compact of hopes and dreams, sustained by its own wonder at itself. The grave call of duty stirs it, love makes it radiant, the passion for truth kindles it with ardor, the adventure of it on an atom of world in the reaches of cosmic loneliness is such as we have no imagination to parallel. The crescent consciousness of being committed to it is, I suspect, what we have so many dull phrases for. It is a tragedy if the issue of it be nothing but dust and darkness.

We shall maintain the glow only as we seek more the more constant sources of it and sensitize our spirits to its finer revelations. We can not keep youth but it is possible to find a compensation for undisciplined dreams in the consciousness of disciplined accomplishment. Memory is no poor substitute for hope. We may always find in our happier recollections something to persuade us that life is rich in gifts and love. The past as well as the future has light and warmth to live by.

"If I were blind, and could no longer see
The lovely vision of a budding tree,

      *   *   *   *   *   *

And if no more my heart could leap to see
The rainbow arch of April's pageantry,

      *   *   *   *   *   *

I should have memories of all these things
That would give blindness sight and darkness wings."

     *   *   *   *   *   *

Very greatly we must seek the glow of life in the sense of the corporate issue of our tasks, finding in the greater things to which we have contributed a heartening compensation for our small part in the result. The mason must see the home through his brick and mortar, the ploughman the harvest beyond his furrows, bread beyond the harvest and beyond the harvest the hungry fed. When the mechanic can say: "I made that motor car," though he only turn a bearing, he will have discovered a secret to touch a lathe with light. Love may wash dishes and keep a home right and lose its romantic rapture in a comradeship which needs no words and still be love.

We shall maintain the glow for ourselves as we keep it alive for others. We were never meant to guard it only for ourselves—that is to lose it. Fathers and mothers find their contentment in the well-being of their children, their glow is no longer self-centered; it is a light which has passed from what heights they have reached to those who follow them, and therein is their peace. It is a woeful thing to cloud the gleam of a child's face or darken the spirit of friend. It is sharing the secret of God to have brought a glow of hope or courage, vision or happiness to others. Our own hearts begin to burn within us as we have done it, and we discover that the glow is never lost by sharing it with another. This is the open secret of keeping it alive.

It must be increasingly sought in the enduring. The great glow is not the property of little fugitive things. It does not rise and fall with the Stock Market, nor attend the fugitive fluctuations of petty success or failure. It belongs to the vision which finds the master values of life, the courage which accepts no defeat as final, the steadfast conscience, the spirit alive to beauty, the love which seeketh not its own, the hope which sees the dawn beyond the dark. It is an aspect of our confidence in the ultimate supremacy of right, the refulgence of a faith which knows that we are not committed by blind force to a meaningless enterprise.

IV

The glow, therefore, which the Apostle exhorts the faithful to maintain is a spiritual glow. He was too wise to leave out that creative word, too searchingly taught of experience. He had seen so many lights darken—youth was gone and station and repute. The issue of his wearing years was, by all the tests of success, pitifully inadequate; he had grown old in sorrow and suffering but his soul was aglow. "I am persuaded," he says, and catalogues every force which could put the glow out to show their powerlessness. He had fought a good fight, he had kept the faith, he awaited the victor's crown. He had maintained a glow to make a prison bright and the lictor's rods an incident in the day's march.

He was the comrade, though they did not know it, of the poets of the Augustan golden age. While he wrote these letters of his a classic literature had taken form whose every fragment the world treasures and yet there was and is a glow in his great passages which no classic literature possesses, an assertion of victory over time and sense, a lyric recitative of the glory of life for which one searches every revelation of the spirit of the Imperial Rome in vain. It was the glow of his soul established in Christian faith and aflame with Christian hope—the reflection of the splendor of the Cross.

The only glow time can not darken is the glow of the soul. The glow *is* the soul. The glow is the light and power of what is best in our natures, it is the way of personality with experience, it *is* courage, it *is* love, it *is* our power to override circumstance. It *is* the wonder of our conscious life, the revelation and force of personality. To maintain that is the task of the soul in time. But the soul needs help. I have said that we maintain the glow by finding it in memory as well as expectation, by looking beyond the details of our tasks to their corporate contributions, by guarding and creating it in others, by transferring it from the transient to the enduring, by making it a quality of our own souls. This is not enough. Unless we live and labor in the persuasion of a vaster love and wisdom for which our lives have meaning, no quality of our own can save the glow from eclipse. It is possible to live bravely without any sureness of the Unseen Comrade. But only the high-spirited are equal to such a challenge and they have left us no testimony of a glowing spirit—only the record of a poignant nobility and the sadness of the tears of things.

Religion is the supreme guardian of the glow and the gleam. It has kept, and keeps, alive the exaltation of spirit without which life is a lonely journey, chilled with apprehension, from the dark to the dark. It invests the temporal with timeless significance, it relates the issues of our little lives to vaster purposes, it sustains the devout in the assurance of an infinite kindness which makes the star-domed universe our Father's house. All religion, shadowed and entangled by human limitations as it has been, has maintained the spiritual glow. Christian faith is in the very nature of it, the one supremely glowing apprehension of life and God. Those who follow its road or rest in its assurance may find shadows enough lying across their paths, but there will always be a light in the heights. There is a warmth of spirit, an unchilled joy in life, a sense of unexhausted wonder in brief days, a persuasion of range and splendor unattained which is nothing else than what the soul brings back from God.

I found the other day in an English periodical a little poem "To An Aviator" by Daniel Whitehead Hickey.

> You who have grown so intimate with stars
> And know their silver dripping from your wings,
> Trod with breaking day across the sky,
> Known kinship with each meteor that sings—
>
> You who have touched the rainbow's fragile gold,
> Carved lyric ways through dawn and dusk and rain
> And soared to heights our hearts have only dreamed—
> How can you walk earth's common ways again?

But how can we walk earth's common ways with a glowing spirit unless we bring to earth-bound things the vision and the comradeship of a region whose lights are kindled by the Eternal? And where shall we find it beyond the power of time or change to dim save in the "way" of Jesus Christ?